THE NEW LIFE

(LA VITA NUOVA)

OF

DANTE ALIGHIERI

TRANSLATED BY

DANTE GABRIEL ROSSETTI

ELLIS AND ELVEY
LONDON
1900

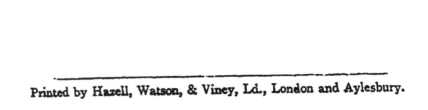

Printed by Hazell, Watson, & Viney, Ld., London and Aylesbury.

PREFATORY NOTE

DANTE GABRIEL ROSSETTI, being the son of an Italian who was greatly immersed in the study of Dante Alighieri, and who produced a Comment on the *Inferno*, and other books relating to Dantesque literature, was from his earliest childhood familiar with the name of the stupendous Florentine, and to some extent aware of the range and quality of his writings. Nevertheless — or perhaps indeed it may have been partly on that very account—he did not in those opening years read Dante to any degree worth mentioning: he was well versed in Shakespeare, Walter Scott, Byron, and some other writers, years before he applied himself to Dante. He may have been fourteen years of age, or even fifteen (May 1843), before he took seriously to the author of the *Divina Commedia*. He then read him eagerly, and with the profoundest admiration and delight; and from the *Commedia* he proceeded to the lyrical poems and the *Vita Nuova.* I question whether he ever read—unless in the most cursory way—other and less fascinating writings of Alighieri, such as the *Convito* and the *De Monarchiâ.*

From reading, Rossetti went on to translating. He translated at an early age, chiefly between 1845 and 1849, a great number of poems by the Italians contemporary with Dante, or preceding him; and, among other things, he made a version of the whole *Vita Nuova,* prose and verse. This may possibly have been the first important thing that he translated from the Italian: if not the first, still less was it the last, and it may well be that his rendering of the book was completed within the year 1846, or early in 1847. He did not, of course, leave his version exactly as it had come at first: on the contrary, he took counsel with friends (Alfred Tennyson among the number), toned down crudities and juvenilities, and worked to make the whole thing impressive and artistic— for in such matters he was much more chargeable with over-fastidiousness than with laxity. Still, the work, as we now have it, is essentially the work of those adolescent years—from time to time reconsidered and improved, but not transmuted.

Some few years after producing his translation of the *Vita Nuova*, Rossetti was desirous of publishing it, and of illustrating the volume with etchings from various designs, which he had meanwhile done, of incidents in the story. This project, however, had to be laid aside, owing to want of means, and the etchings were never undertaken. It was only in 1861 that the volume named *The Early Italian Poets*, including the translated *Vita Nuova*, was brought out : the same volume, with a change in the arrangement of its contents, was reissued in 1874, entitled *Dante and his Circle*. This book, in its original form, was received with favour, and settled the claim of Rossetti to rank as a poetic translator, or indeed as a poet in his own right.

For *The Early Italian Poets* he wrote a Preface, from which a passage, immediately relating to the *Vita Nuova*, is extracted in the present edition. There are some other passages, affecting the whole of the translations in that volume, which deserve to be borne in mind, as showing the spirit in which he undertook the translating work, and I give them here :—

"The life-blood of rhythmical translation is this commandment—that a good poem shall not be turned into a bad one. The only true motive for putting poetry into a fresh language must be to endow a fresh nation, as far as possible, with one more possession of beauty. Poetry not being an exact science, literality of rendering is altogether secondary to this chief law. I say *literality*,—not fidelity, which is by no means the same thing. When literality can be combined with what is thus the primary condition of success, the translator is fortunate, and must strive his utmost to unite them ; when such object can only be obtained by paraphrase, that is his only path. Any merit possessed by these translations is derived from an effort to follow this principle. . . . The task of the translator (and with all humility be it spoken) is one of some self-denial. Often would he avail himself of any special grace of his own idiom and epoch, if only his will belonged to him : often would some cadence serve him but for his author's structure — some structure but for his author's cadence : often the beautiful turn of a stanza must be weakened to adopt some rhyme which will tally, and he sees the poet revelling in abundance of language where himself is scantily supplied. Now he would slight the matter for the music, and now the music for the matter ; but no, he must deal to each alike. Sometimes too a flaw in the work galls him, and he would fain remove it, doing for the poet that which his age denied him ; but no, it is not in the bond."

It may be as well to explain here a very small share which I myself took in the *Vita Nuova* translation. When the volume *The Early Italian Poets* was in preparation, my brother asked me (January 1861) to aid by "collating my *Vita Nuova* with the original, and amending inaccuracies." He defined the work further as follows : "What I want is that you should correct my translation throughout, removing inaccuracies and mannerisms. And, if you have time, it would be a great service to translate the analyses of the poems (which I omitted). This, however, if you think it desirable to include them. I did not at the time (on ground of readableness), but since think

they may be desirable : only have become so un-
familiar with the book that I have no distinct
opinion." On January 25th he wrote : "Many
and many thanks for a most essential service most
thoroughly performed. I have not yet verified
the whole of the notes, but I see they are just
what I needed, and will save me a vast amount
of trouble. I should very much wish that the
translation were more literal, but cannot do it all
again. *My* notes, which you have taken the
trouble of revising, are, of course, quite paltry and
useless."

In order that the reader may judge as to this
question of literality, I will give here the literal
Englishing of the Sonnet at p. 38, and the para-
graph which precedes it (I take the passage quite
at random), and the reader can, if he likes, com-
pare this rendering with that which appears in
Dante Rossetti's text :—

"After the departure of this gentlewoman it was
the pleasure of the Lord of the Angels to call to
His glory a lady young and much of noble * aspect,

---

* *Gentile.* The word means ''noble'' rather than (in
its modern shade of meaning) ''gentle.'' ''Genteel'' would

who was very graceful in this aforesaid city : whose body I saw lying without the soul amid many ladies, who were weeping very piteously. Then, remembering that erewhile I had seen her keeping company with that most noble one, I could not withhold some tears. Indeed, weeping, I purposed to speak certain words about her death, in guerdon of my having at some whiles seen her with my lady. And somewhat of this I referred to in the last part of the words which I spoke of her, as manifestly appears to him who understands them : and then I composed these two Sonnets—of which the first begins, 'Weep, lovers'—the second, 'Villain Death.'

"Weep, lovers, since Love weeps,—hearkening what cause makes him wail : Love hears ladies invoking pity, showing bitter grief outwardly by the eyes ; because villain Death has set his cruel working upon a noble heart, ruining that which in a noble lady is to be praised in the world, apart from honour. Hear how much Love did her honouring ; for I saw him lamenting in very

sometimes apply, but has ceased to be admissible in serious writing.

person over the dead seemly image : and often he gazed towards heaven, wherein was already settled the noble soul who had been a lady of such gladsome semblance."

It would be out of place to enter here into any detailed observations upon the *Vita Nuova*, its meaning, and the literature which has grown out of it. I will merely name, as obvious things for the English reader to consult, the translation which was made by Sir Theodore Martin ; the essay by Professor C. Eliot Norton ; the translations published by Dr. Garnett in his book entitled *Dante, Petrarch, Camoens, 124 Sonnets*, along with the remarks in his valuable *History of Italian Literature*; Scartazzini's *Companion to Dante*; and the publications of the Rev. Dr. Moore, the foremost of our living Dante scholars.

W. M. ROSSETTI.

August 1899.

INTRODUCTION.

THE *Vita Nuova* (the Autobiography or Auto-psychology of Dante's youth till about his twenty-seventh year) is already well known to many in the original, or by means of essays and of English versions partial or entire. It is therefore, and on all accounts, unnecessary to say much more of the work here than it says for itself. Wedded to its exquisite and intimate beauties are personal peculiarities which excite wonder and conjecture, best replied to in the words which Beatrice herself is made to utter in the *Commedia* : "Questi *fù tal* nella sua vita nuova."* Thus then young Dante *was*. All that seemed possible to be done here for the work was to translate it in as free and clear a form as was consistent

* "Purgatorio," C. xxx.

with fidelity to its meaning; and to ease it, as far
as possible, from notes and encumbrances.

It may be noted here how necessary a knowledge
of the *Vita Nuova* is to the full comprehension of
the part borne by Beatrice in the *Commedia*. More-
over, it is only from the perusal of its earliest and
then undivulged self-communings that we can
divine the whole bitterness of wrong to such a
soul as Dante's, its poignant sense of abandonment,
or its deep and jealous refuge in memory. Above
all, it is here that we find the first manifestations
of that wisdom of obedience, that natural breath
of duty, which afterwards, in the *Commedia*, lifted
up a mighty voice for warning and testimony.
Throughout the *Vita Nuova* there is a strain like
the first falling murmur which reaches the ear
in some remote meadow, and prepares us to look
upon the sea.

Boccaccio, in his Life of Dante, tells us that the

great poet, in later life, was ashamed of this work
of his youth. Such a statement hardly seems
reconcilable with the allusions to it made or implied
in the *Commedia*; but it is true that the *Vita Nuova*
is a book which only youth could have produced,
and which must chiefly remain sacred to the young ;
to each of whom the figure of Beatrice, less lifelike
than lovelike, will seem the friend of his own heart.
Nor is this, perhaps, its least praise. To tax its
author with effeminacy on account of the extreme
sensitiveness evinced by this narrative of his love,
would be manifestly unjust, when we find that,
though love alone is the theme of the *Vita Nuova*,
war already ranked among its author's experiences
at the period to which it relates. In the year 1289,
the one preceding the death of Beatrice, Dante
served with the foremost cavalry in the great
battle of Campaldino, on the eleventh of June,
when the Florentines defeated the people of Arezzo,

In the autumn of the next year, 1290, when for him, by the death of Beatrice, the city as he says "sat solitary," such refuge as he might find from his grief was sought in action and danger: for we learn from the *Commedia* (Hell, C. xxi.) that he served in the war then waged by Florence upon Pisa, and was present at the surrender of Caprona. He says, using the reminiscence to give life to a description, in his great way:—

" I've seen the troops out of Caprona go
    On terms, affrighted thus, when on the spot
They found themselves with foemen compass'd so.'

(CAYLEY'S *Translation*.)

A word should be said here of the title of Dante's autobiography. The adjective *Nuovo, nuova*, or *Novello, novella*, literally *New*, is often used by Dante and other early writers in the sense of *young*. This has induced some editors of the *Vita Nuova* to explain the title as meaning

Early Life. I should be glad on some accounts to adopt this supposition, as everything is a gain which increases clearness to the modern reader; but on consideration I think the more mystical interpretation of the words, as *New Life* (in reference to that revulsion of his being which Dante so minutely describes as having occurred simultaneously with his first sight of Beatrice), appears the primary one, and therefore the most necessary to be given in a translation. The probability may be that both were meant, but this I cannot convey.*

* I must hazard here (to relieve the first page of my translation from a long note) a suggestion as to the meaning of the most puzzling passage in the whole *Vita Nuova,*— that sentence just at the outset which says, "La gloriosa donna della mia mente, la quale fù chiamata da molti Beatrice, i quali non sapeano che si chiamare." On this passage all the commentators seem helpless, turning it about and sometimes adopting alterations not to be found in any ancient manuscript of the work. The words mean

literally, "The glorious lady of my mind who was called Beatrice by many who knew not how she was called." This presents the obvious difficulty that the lady's name really *was* Beatrice, and that Dante throughout uses that name himself. In the text of my version I have adopted, as a rendering, the one of the various compromises which seemed to give the most beauty to the meaning. But it occurs to me that a less irrational escape out of the difficulty than any I have seen suggested may possibly be found by linking this passage with the close of the sonnet at page 104 of the *Vita Nuova*, beginning, "I felt a spirit of love begin to stir," in the last line of which sonnet Love is made to assert that the name of Beatrice is *Love*. Dante appears to have dwelt on this fancy with some pleasure, from what is said in an earlier sonnet (page 39) about "Love in his proper form" (by which Beatrice seems to be meant) bending over a dead lady. And it is in connection with the sonnet where the name of Beatrice is said to be Love, that Dante, as if to show us that the Love he speaks of is only his own emotion, enters into an argument as to Love being merely an accident in substance,—in other words, "Amore e il cor gentil son una cosa." This conjecture may be pronounced extravagant ; but the *Vita Nuova*, when examined, proves so full of intricate and fantastic analogies, even in the mere arrangement of its parts, (much more than appears on any but the closest scrutiny,) that it seems admissible to suggest even a whimsical solution of a difficulty which remains unconquered.   Or to have recourse to the much more welcome means of solution afforded by simple inherent beauty : may not the meaning be merely that any person looking on so noble and lovely a creation, without knowledge of her name, must have spontaneously called her Beatrice,— *i.e.*, the giver of blessing? This would be analogous by antithesis to the translation I have adopted in my text.

DANTE ALIGHIERI

THE NEW LIFE.

(LA VITA NUOVA.)

IN that part of the book of my memory before the which is little that can be read, there is a rubric, saying, *Incipit Vita Nova.** Under such rubric I find written many things; and among them the words which I purpose to copy into this little book; if not all of them, at the least their substance.

Nine times already since my birth had the heaven of light returned to the selfsame point almost, as concerns its own revolution, when first the glorious Lady of my mind was made manifest to mine eyes; even she who was called Beatrice by many who knew

* " Here beginneth the new life."

not wherefore. * She had already been in this life for so long as that, within her time, the starry heaven had moved towards the Eastern quarter one of the twelve parts of a degree ; so that she appeared to me at the beginning of her ninth year almost, and I saw her almost at the end of my ninth year. Her dress, on that day, was of a most noble colour, a subdued and goodly crimson, girdled and adorned in such sort as best suited with her very tender age. At that moment, I say most truly that the spirit of life, which hath its dwelling in the secretest chamber of the heart, began to tremble so violently that the least pulses of my body shook therewith ; and in trembling it said these words : *Ecce deus fortior me,*

* In reference to the meaning of the name, "She who confers blessing." We learn from Boccaccio that this first meeting took place at a May Feast, given in the year 1274 by Folco Portinari, father of Beatrice, who ranked among the principal citizens of Florence : to which feast Dante accompanied his father, Alighiero Alighieri.

Religious significance? Beacon toward Absolution, as $3^3 = 9$ trinity.

*qui veniens dominabitur mihi.** At that moment the animate spirit, which dwelleth in the lofty chamber whither all the senses carry their perceptions, was filled with wonder, and speaking more especially unto the spirits of the eyes, said these words: *Apparuit iam beatitudo vestra.*† At that moment the natural spirit, which dwelleth there where our nourishment is administered, began to weep, and in weeping said these words: *Heu miser! quia frequenter mpeditus ero deinceps.*‡

I say that, from that time forward, Love quite governed my soul; which was immediately espoused to him, and with so safe and undisputed a lordship (by virtue of strong imagination) that I had nothing left for it but to do all his bidding continually. He

* "Here is a deity stronger than I; who, coming, shall rule over me."

† "Your beatitude hath now been made manifest unto you."

‡ "Woe is me! for that often I shall be disturbed from this time forth!"

oftentimes commanded me to seek if I might see this youngest of he Angels: wherefore I in my boyhood often went in search of her, and found her so noble and praiseworthy that certainly of her might have been said hose words of the poet Homer, "She seemed not to be the daughter of a mortal man, but of God."* And albeit her image, that was with me always, was an exultation of Love to subdue me, it was yet of so perfect a quality that it never allowed me to be overruled by Love without the faithful counsel of reason, whensoever such counsel was useful to be heard. But seeing that were I to dwell overmuch on the passions and doings of such early youth, my words might be counted something fabulous, I will therefore put them aside; and passing many things that may be conceived by the

Homer

---

* Οὐδὲ ἐῴκει
Ανδρός γε θνητοῦ παῖς ἔμμεναι, ἀλλὰ θεοῖο.

(*Iliad*, xxiv. 258.)

pattern of these, I will come to such as are writ in my memory with a better distinctness.

After the lapse of so many days that nine years exactly were completed since the above-written appearance of this most gracious being, on the last of those days it happened that the same wonderful lady appeared to me dressed all in pure white, between two gentle ladies elder than she. And passing through a street, she turned her eyes thither where I stood sorely abashed : and by her unspeakable courtesy, which is now guerdoned in the Great Cycle, she saluted me with so virtuous a bearing that I seemed then and there to behold the very limits of blessedness. The hour of her most sweet salutation was exactly the ninth of that day; and because it was the first time that any words from her reached mine ears, I came into such sweetness that I parted thence as one intoxicated. And betaking me to the loneliness of mine own room, I fell to thinking of

2) Overwhelmed and intoxicated by her presence

this most courteous lady, thinking of whom I was overtaken by a pleasant slumber, wherein a marvellous vision was presented to me : for there appeared to be in my room a mist of the colour of fire, within the which I discerned the figure of a lord of terrible aspect to such as should gaze upon him, but who seemed therewithal to rejoice inwardly that it was a marvel to see. Speaking he said many things, among the which I could understand but few; and of these, this : *Ego dominus uus.** In his arms it seemed to me that a person was sleeping, covered only with a blood-coloured cloth ; upon whom looking very attentively, I knew that it was the lady of the salutation who had deigned the day before to salute me. And he who held her held also in his hand a thing that was burning in flames ; and he said to me, *Vide cor tuum.*† But when he had

* "I am thy master."
† "Behold thy heart."

remained with me a little while, I thought that he set himself to awaken her that slept; after the which he made her to eat that thing which flamed in his hand; and she ate as one fearing. Then, having waited again a space, all his joy was turned into most bitter weeping; and as he wept he gathered the lady into his arms, and it seemed to me that he went with her up towards heaven: whereby such a great anguish came upon me that my light slumber could not endure through it, but was suddenly broken. And immediately having considered, I knew that the hour wherein this vision had been made manifest to me was the fourth hour (which is to say, the first of the nine last hours) of the night.

Then, musing on what I had seen, I proposed to relate the same to many poets who were famous in that day: and for that I had myself in some sort the art of discoursing with rhyme, I resolved on making a sonnet, in the which, having saluted all

such as are subject unto Love, and entreated them
to expound my vision, I should write unto them
those things which I had seen in my sleep. And
the sonnet I made was this : —

To every heart which the sweet pain doth move,
   And unto which these words may now be brought
   For true interpretation and kind thought,
Be greeting in our Lord's name, which is Love.
Of those long hours wherein the stars, above,
   Wake and keep watch, the third was almost nought,
   When Love was shown me with such terrors fraught
As may not carelessly be spoken of.
He seemed like one who is full of joy, and had
   My heart within his hand, and on his arm
    My lady, with a mantle round her, slept;
Whom (having wakened her) anon he made
   To eat that heart; she ate, as fearing harm.
    Then he went out; and as he went, he wept.

This sonnet is divided into two parts. In the first part I give greeting, and ask an answer; in the second, I signify what thing has to be answered to. The second part commences here: "Of those long hours."

To this sonnet I received many answers, conveying many different opinions; of the which one was sent by him whom I now call the first among my friends, and it began thus, "Unto my thinking thou beheld'st all worth."* And indeed, it was when he learned that I was he who had sent those rhymes to him, that our friendship commenced. But the true meaning of that vision was not then perceived by any one, though it be now evident to the least skilful.

From that night forth, the natural functions of my

---

* The friend of whom Dante here speaks was Guido Cavalcanti.

body began to be vexed and impeded, for I was given up wholly to thinking of this most gracious creature: whereby in short space I became so weak and so reduced that it was irksome to many of my friends to look upon me; while others, being moved by spite, went about to discover what it was my wish should be concealed. Wherefore I (perceiving the drift of their unkindly questions), by Love's will, who directed me according to the counsels of reason, told them how it was Love himself who had thus dealt with me: and I said so, because the thing was so plainly to be discerned in my countenance that there was no longer any means of concealing it. But when they went on to ask, "And by whose help hath Love done this?" I looked in their faces smiling, and spake no word in return.

Now it fell on a day, that this most gracious creature was sitting where words were to be heard

of the Queen of Glory;* and I was in a place
whence mine eyes could behold their beatitude:
and betwixt her and me, in a direct line, there
sat another lady of a pleasant favour; who looked
round at me many times, marvelling at my continued
gaze which seemed to have *her* for its object.
And many perceived that she thus looked; so that
departing thence, I heard it whispered after me,
"Look you to what a pass *such a lady* hath brought
him;" and in saying this they named her who
had been midway between the most gentle Beatrice
and mine eyes. Therefore I was reassured, and
knew that for that day my secret had not become
manifest. Then immediately it came into my
mind that I might make use of this lady as a
screen to the truth: and so well did I play my part
that the most of those who had hitherto watched and
wondered at me, now imagined they had found

* *i.e.*, in a church.

me out. By her means I kept my secret concealed till some years were gone over; and for my better security, I even made divers rhymes in her honour; whereof I shall here write only as much as concerneth the most gentle Beatrice, which is but a very little. Moreover, about the same time while this lady was a screen for so much love on my part, I took the resolution to set down the name of this most gracious creature accompanied with many other women's names, and especially with hers whom I spake of. And to this end I put together the names of sixty of the most beautiful ladies in that city where God had placed mine own lady; and these names I introduced in an epistle in the form of a *sirvent*, which it is not my intention to transcribe here. Neither should I have said anything of this matter, did I not wish to take note of a certain strange thing, to wit: that having written the list, I found my lady's name would not stand otherwise than ninth in order among the names of these ladies.

Now it so chanced with her by whose means I had thus long time concealed my desire, that it behoved her to leave the city I speak of, and to journey afar: wherefore I, being sorely perplexed at the loss of so excellent a defence, had more trouble than even I could before have supposed. And thinking that if I spoke not somewhat mournfully of her departure, my former counterfeiting would be the more quickly perceived, I determined that I would make a grievous sonnet * thereof; the which I will write here, because it hath certain words in it whereof my lady was the immediate

---

* It will be observed that this poem is not what we now call a sonnet. Its structure, however, is analogous to that of the sonnet, being two sextetts followed by two quatrains, instead of two quatrains followed by two triplets. Dante applies the term sonnet to both these forms of composition, and to no other.

cause, as will be plain to him that understands.
And the sonnet was this :—

ALL ye that pass along Love's trodden way,
Pause ye awhile and say
   If there be any grief like unto mine:
I pray you that you hearken a short space
Patiently, if my case
   Be not a piteous marvel and a sign.

Love (never, certes, for my worthless part,
But of his own great heart,)
   Vouchsafed to me a life so calm and sweet
That oft I heard folk question as I went
What such great gladness meant :—
   They spoke of it behind me in the street.

But now that fearless bearing is all gone
   Which with Love's hoarded wealth was given me;
   Till I am grown to be
So poor that I have dread to think thereon.

And thus it is that I, being like as one
Who is ashamed and hides his poverty,
Without seem full of glee,
And let my heart within travail and moan.

*This poem has two principal parts; for, in the
first, I mean to call the Faithful of Love in those
words of Jeremias the Prophet,* "O vos omnes qui
transitis per viam, attendite et videte si est dolor
sicut dolor meus," *and to pray them to stay and hear
me. In the second I tell where Love had placed
me, with a meaning other than that which the
last part of the poem shows, and I say what I
have lost. The second part begins here,* "*Love,
(never, certes).*"

A certain while after the departure of that lady,
it pleased the Master of the Angels to call into
His glory a damsel, young and of a gentle
presence, who had been very lovely in the city

I speak of: and I saw her body lying without
its soul among many ladies, who held a pitiful
weeping. Whereupon, remembering that I had seen
her in the company of excellent Beatrice, I could
not hinder myself from a few tears; and weeping,
I conceived to say somewhat of her death, in
guerdon of having seen her somewhile with my
lady; which thing I spake of in the latter end
of the verses that I writ in this matter, as he
will discern who understands. And I wrote two
sonnets, which are these :—

I.

WEEP, Lovers, sith Love's very self doth weep,
   And sith the cause for weeping is so great;
   When now so many dames, of such estate
In worth, show with their eyes a grief so deep :
For Death the churl has laid his leaden sleep
   Upon a damsel who was fair of late,

Defacing all our earth should celebrate,—

Yea all save virtue, which the soul doth keep.

Now hearken how much Love did honour her.

　I myself saw him in his proper form

　　Bending above the motionless sweet dead,

And often gazing into Heaven; for there

　The soul now sits which when her life was
　　warm

　　Dwelt with the joyful beauty that is fled.

This first sonnet is divided into three parts. In the first, I call and beseech the Faithful of Love to weep; and I say that their Lord weeps, and that they, hearing the reason why he weeps, shall be more minded to listen to me. In the second, I relate this reason. In the third, I speak of honour done by Love to this Lady. The second part begins here, " When now so many dames;" the third here, " Now hearken."

II.

DEATH, alway cruel, Pity's foe in chief,
Mother who brought forth grief,
   Merciless judgment and without appeal!
   Since thou alone hast made my heart to feel
   This sadness and unweal,
My tongue upbraideth thee without relief.

And now (for I must rid thy name of ruth)
Behoves me speak the truth
   Touching thy cruelty and wickedness:
   Not that they be not known; but ne'ertheless
   I would give hate more stress
With them that feed on love in very sooth.

Out of this world thou nast driven courtesy,
   And virtue, dearly prized in womanhood;
   And out of youth's gay mood
The lovely lightness is quite gone through thee.

Whom now I mourn, no man shall learn from me
Save by the measure of these praises given.
Whoso deserves not Heaven
May never hope to have her company.*

This poem is divided into four parts. In the first I address Death by certain proper names of hers. In the second, speaking to her, I tell the reason why I am moved to denounce her. In the third, I rail against her. In the fourth, I turn to speak to a person undefined, although defined in my own conception. The second part commences here, "Since thou alone;" the third here, "And now (for I must);" the fourth here, "Whoso deserves not."

* The commentators assert that the last two lines here do not allude to the dead lady, but to Beatrice. This would make the poem very clumsy in construction; yet there must be some covert allusion to Beatrice, as Dante himself intimates. The only form in which I can trace it consists in the implied assertion that such person as *had* enjoyed the dead lady's

Some days after the death of this lady, I had oc-
casion to leave the city I speak of, and to go thither-
wards where she abode who had formerly been my
protection; albeit the end of my journey reached
not altogether so far. And notwithstanding that I
was visibly in the company of many, the journey
was so irksome that I had scarcely sighing enough
to ease my heart's heaviness; seeing that as I
went, I left my beatitude behind me. Wherefore
it came to pass that he who ruled me by virtue of
my most gentle lady was made visible to my mind,
in the light habit of a traveller, coarsely fashioned.
He appeared to me troubled, and looked always on

society was worthy of heaven, and that person was Beatrice.
Or indeed the allusion to Beatrice might be in the first poem,
where he says that Love " *in forma vera* " (that is, Beatrice),
mourned over the corpse : as he afterwards says of Beatrice,
" *Quella ha nome Amor.*"   Most probably *both* allusions are
intended.

the ground; saving only that sometimes his eyes were turned towards a river which was clear and rapid, and which flowed along the path I was taking. And then I thought that Love called me and said to me these words: "I come from that lady who was so long thy surety; for the matter of whose return, I know that it may not be. Wherefore I have taken that heart which I made thee leave with her, and do bear it unto another lady, who, as she was, shall be thy surety;" (and when he named her I knew her well). "And of these words I have spoken, if thou shouldst speak any again, let it be in such sort as that none shall perceive thereby that thy love was feigned for her, which thou must now feign for another." And when he had spoken thus, all my imagining was gone suddenly, for it seemed to me that Love became a part of myself: so that, changed as it were in mine aspect, I rode on full of thought the

whole of that day, and with heavy sighing. And
the day being over, I wrote this sonnet :—

A DAY agone, as I rode sullenly
  Upon a certain path that liked me not,
  I met Love midway while the air was hot,
Clothed lightly as a wayfarer might be.
And for the cheer he showed, he seemed to me
  As one who hath lost lordship he had got ;
  Advancing tow'rds me full of sorrowful thought,
Bowing his forehead so that none should see.
Then as I went, he called me by my name,
  Sayin : "I journey since the morn was dim
    Thence where I made thy heart to be : which
    now
I needs must bear unto another dame."
  Wherewith so much passed into me of him
  That he was gone, and I discerned not how.

This sonnet has three parts. In the first part,

I tell how I met Love, and of his aspect. In the second, I tell what he said to me, although not in full, through the fear I had of discovering my secret. In the third, I say how he disappeared. The second part commences here, "Then as I went;" the third here, "Wherewith so much."

On my return, I set myself to seek out that lady whom my master had named to me while I journeyed sighing. And because I would be brief, I will now narrate that in a short while I made her my surety, in such sort that the matter was spoken of by many in terms scarcely courteous; through the which I had oftenwhiles many troublesome hours. And by this it happened (to wit: by this false and evil rumour which seemed to misfame me of vice) that she who was the destroyer of all evil and the queen of all good, coming where I was, denied me her most sweet salutation, in the which alone was my blessedness.

And here it is fitting for me to depart a little from this present matter, that it may be rightly understood of what surpassing virtue her salutation was to me. To the which end I say that when she appeared in any place, it seemed to me, by the hope of her excellent salutation, that there was no man mine enemy any longer; and such warmth of charity came upon me that most certainly in that moment I would have pardoned whosoever had done me an injury; and if one should then have questioned me concerning any matter, I could only have said unto him "Love," with a countenance clothed in humbleness. And what time she made ready to salute me, the spirit of Love, destroying all other perceptions, thrust forth the feeble spirits of my eyes, saying, "Do homage unto your mistress," and putting itself in their place to obey: so that he who would, might then have beheld Love, beholding the lids of mine eyes shake. And when this most gentle lady gave her salutation, Love, so far from being a medium beclouding mine intolerable beatitude, then bred in me such an overpowering sweetness that my body, being all subjected thereto, remained many times helpless and passive. Whereby it is made manifest that in her salutation alone was there any beatitude for me, which then very often went beyond my endurance.

And now, resuming my discourse, I will go on to relate that when, for the first time, this beatitude was denied me, I became possessed with such grief that, parting myself from others, I went into a lonely place to bathe the ground with most bitter tears : and when, by this heat of weeping, I was somewhat relieved, I betook myself to my chamber, where I could lament unheard. And there, having prayed to the Lady of all Mercies, and having said also, "O Love, aid thou thy servant," I went suddenly asleep like a beaten sobbing child. And in my sleep,

towards the middle of it, I seemed to see in the
room, seated at my side, a youth in very white
raiment, who kept his eyes fixed on me in deep
thought. And when he had gazed some time, I
thought that he sighed and called to me in these
words: "*Fili mi, tempus est ut prætermittantur
simulata nostra.*" * And thereupon I seemed to
know him; for the voice was the same wherewith
he had spoken at other times in my sleep. Then
looking at him, I perceived that· he was weeping
piteously, and that he seemed to be waiting for me
to speak. Wherefore, taking heart, I began thus:
"Why weepest thou, Master of all honour?" And
he made answer to me: "*Ego tanquam centrum
circuli, cui simili modo se habent circumferentiæ
partes: tu autem non sic.*"† And thinking upon

* "My son, it is time for us to lay aside our counterfeiting."
† "I am as the centre of a circle, to the which all parts
of the circumference bear an equal relation: but with thee

his words, they seemed to me obscure; so that again compelling myself unto speech, I asked of him: "What thing is this, Master, that thou hast spoken thus darkly?" To the which he made answer in the vulgar tongue: "Demand no more than may be useful to thee." Whereupon I began to discourse with him concerning her salutation which she had

---

it is not thus." This phrase seems to have remained as obscure to commentators as Dante found it at the moment. No one, as far as I know, has even fairly tried to find a meaning for it. To me the following appears a not unlikely one. Love is weeping on Dante's account, and not on his own. He says, "I am the centre of a circle *(Amor che muove il sole e l' altre stelle):* therefore all lovable objects, whether in heaven or earth, or any part of the circle's circumference, are equally near to me. Not so thou, who wilt one day lose Beatrice when she goes to heaven." The phrase would thus contain an intimation of the death of Beatrice, accounting for Dante being next told not to inquire the meaning of the speech,—"Demand no more than may be useful to thee."

denied me; and when I had questioned him of the cause, he said these words: "Our Beatrice hath heard from certain persons, that the lady whom I named to thee while thou journeyedst full of sighs is sorely disquieted by thy solicitations: and therefore this most gracious creature, who is the enemy of all disquiet, being fearful of such disquiet, refused to salute thee. For the which reason (albeit, in very sooth, thy secret must needs have become known to her by familiar observation) it is my will that thou compose certain things in rhyme, in the which thou shalt set forth how strong a mastership I have obtained over thee, through her; and how thou wast hers even from thy childhood. Also do thou call upon him that knoweth these things to bear witness to them, bidding him to speak with her thereof; the which I, who am he, will do willingly. And thus she shall be made to know thy desire; knowing which, she shall know likewise that they were deceived who spake of thee to her. And so write these things, that they shall seem rather to be spoken by a third person; and not directly by thee to her, which is scarce fitting. After the which, send them, not without me, where she may chance to hear them; but have them fitted with a pleasant music, into the which I will pass whensoever it needeth." With this speech he was away, and my sleep was broken up.

Whereupon, remembering me, I knew that I had beheld this vision during the ninth hour of the day; and I resolved that I would make a ditty, before I left my chamber, according to the words my master had spoken. And this is the ditty that I made :—

Song, 'tis my will that thou do seek out Love,
    And go with him where my dear lady is;
    That so my cause, the which thy harmonies
Do plead, his better speech may clearly prove.

Thou goest, my Song, in such a courteous kind,
  That even companionless
    Thou mayst rely on thyself anywhere.
And yet, an thou wouldst get thee a safe mind,
  First unto Love address
    Thy steps; whose aid, mayhap, 'twere ill to spare,
    Seeing that she to whom thou mak'st thy prayer
Is, as I think, ill-minded unto me,
And that if Love do not companion thee,
  Thou'lt have perchance small cheer to tell me of.

With a sweet accent, when thou com'st to her,
  Begin thou in these words,
    First having craved a gracious audience:
"He who hath sent me as his messenger,
  Lady, thus much records,
    An thou but suffer him, in his defence.
    Love, who comes with me, by thine influence
Can make this man do as it liketh him:

Wherefore, if this fault *is* or doth but *seem*
  Do thou conceive : for his heart cannot move."

Say to her also : "Lady, his poor heart
  Is so confirmed in faith
    That all its thoughts are but of serving thee :
'Twas early thine, and could not swerve apart."
  Then, if she wavereth,
    Bid her ask Love, who knows if these things be.
    And in the end, beg of her modestly
To pardon so much boldness : saying too :—
" If thou declare his death to be thy due,
  The thing shall come to pass, as doth behove."

Then pray thou of the Master of all ruth,
  Before thou leave her there,
    That he befriend my cause and plead it well.
" In guerdon of my sweet rhymes and my truth"
  (Entreat him) "stay with her ;
    Let not the hope of thy poor servant fail ;

And if with her thy pleading should prevail,
Let her look on him and give peace to him."
Gentle my Song, if good to thee it seem,
Do this : so worship shall be thine and love.

This ditty is divided into three parts. In the first, I tell it whither to go, and I encourage it, that it may go the more confidently, and I tell it whose company to join if it would go with confidence and without any danger. In the second, I say that which it behoves the ditty to set forth. In the third, I give it leave to start when it pleases, recommending its course to the arms of Fortune. The second part begins here, " With a sweet accent;" the third here, " Gentle my Song." Some might contradict me, and say that they understand not whom I address in the second person, seeing that the ditty is merely the very words I am speaking. And therefore I say that this doubt I intend to solve and clear up in

this little book itself, at a more difficult passage,
and then let him understand who now doubts, or
would now contradict as aforesaid.

After this vision I have recorded, and having
written those words which Love had dictated to
me, I began to be harassed with many and divers
thoughts, by each of which I was sorely tempted;
and in especial, there were four among them that
left me no rest. The first was this: "Certainly the
lordship of Love is good; seeing that it diverts
the mind from all mean things." The second was
this: "Certainly the lordship of Love is evil;
seeing that the more homage his servants pay to
him, the more grievous and painful are the torments
wherewith he torments them." The third was
this: "The name of Love is so sweet in the hearing
that it would not seem possible for its effects to
be other than sweet; seeing that the name must
needs be like unto the thing named; as it is

written : *Nomina sunt consequentia rerum.*"* And the fourth was this : "The lady whom Love hath chosen out to govern thee is not as other ladies, whose hearts are easily moved."

And by each one of these thoughts I was so sorely assailed that I was like unto him who doubteth which path to take, and wishing to go, goeth not. And if I bethought myself to seek out some point at the which all these paths might be found to meet, I discerned but one way, and that irked me ; to wit, to call upon Pity, and to commend myself. unto her. And it was then that, feeling a desire to write somewhat thereof in rhyme, I wrote this sonnet :—

ALL my thoughts always speak to me of Love,
    Yet have between themselves such difference
    That while one bids me bow with mind and sense,
A second saith, "Go to : look thou above ; "

* " Names are the consequents of things."

The third one, hoping, yields me joy en′

  And with the last come tears, I scarce k

  All of them craving pity in sore suspense,

Trembling with fears that the heart knoweth of.

And thus, being all unsure which path to take,

  Wishing to speak I know not what to say,

    And lose myself in amorous wanderings :

Until, (my peace with all of them to make,)

  Unto mine enemy I needs must pray,

    My Lady Pity, for the help she brings.

This sonnet may be divided into four parts. In the first, I say and propound that all my thoughts are concerning Love. In the second, I say that they are diverse, and I relate their diversity. In the third, I say wherein they all seem to agree. In the fourth, I say that, wishing to speak of Love, I know not from which of these thoughts to take my argument; and that if I would take it from all, I

shall have to call upon mine enemy, my Lady Pity.
"Lady" I say, as in a scornful mode of speech.
The second begins here, "Yet have between them-
selves;" the third, "All of them craving;" the
fourth, "And thus."

After this battling with many thoughts, it chanced
on a day that my most gracious lady was with
a gathering of ladies in a certain place; to the
which I was conducted by a friend of mine; he
thinking to do me a great pleasure by showing
me the beauty of so many women. Then I,
hardly knowing whereunto he conducted me, but
trusting in him (who yet was leading his friend to
the last verge of life), made question: "To what
end are we come among these ladies?" and he
answered: "To the end that they may be worthily
served." And they were assembled around a
gentlewoman who was given in marriage on that
day; the custom of the city being that these should

bear her company when she sat down for the first time at table in the house of her husband. Therefore I, as was my friend's pleasure, resolved to stay with him and do honour to those ladies.

But as soon as I had thus resolved, I began to feel a faintness and a throbbing at my left side, which soon took possession of my whole body. Whereupon I remember that I covertly leaned my back unto a painting that ran round the walls of that house; and being fearful lest my trembling should be discerned of them, I lifted mine eyes to look on those ladies, and then first perceived among them the excellent Beatrice. And when I perceived her, all my senses were overpowered by the great lordship that Love obtained, finding himself so near unto that most gracious being, until nothing but the spirits of sight remained to me; and even these remained driven out of their own instruments because Love entered in that honoured

place of theirs, that so he might the better
behold her. And although I was other than at first,
I grieved for the spirits so expelled, which kept up
a sore lament, saying : " If he had not in this
wise thrust us forth, we also should behold the
marvel of this lady." By this, many of her friends,
having discerned my confusion, began to wonder ;
and together with herself, kept whispering of me
and mocking me. Whereupon my friend, who knew
not what to conceive, took me by the hands, and
drawing me forth from among them, required to know
what ailed me. Then, having first held me at quiet
for a space until my perceptions were come back
to me, I made answer to my friend : "Of a surety
I have now set my feet on that point of life,
beyond the which he must not pass who would
return." *

* It is difficult not to connect Dante's agony at this wedding-
feast with our knowledge that in her twenty-first year Beatrice

Afterwards, leaving him, I went back to the room where I had wept before; and again weeping and ashamed, said: "It this lady but knew of my condition, I do not think that she would thus mock at me; nay, I am sure that she must needs feel some pity." And in my weeping I bethought me to write certain words, in the which, speaking to her, I should signify the occasion of my disfigurement, telling her also how I knew that she had no knowledge thereof: which, if it were known, I was certain must move others to pity. And then, because I hoped that peradventure

was wedded to Simone de' Bardi. That she herself was the bride on this occasion might seem out of the question, from the fact of its not being in any way so stated: but on the other hand, Dante's silence throughout the *Vita Nuova* as regards her marriage (which must have brought deep sorrow even to his ideal love) is so startling, that we might almost be led to conceive in this passage the only intimation of it which he thought fit to give.

it might come into her hearing, I wrote this
sonnet :—

EVEN as the others mock, thou mockest me ;
  Not dreaming, noble lady, whence it is
  That I am taken with strange semblances,
Seeing thy face which is so fair to see :
For else, compassion would not suffer thee
  To grieve my heart with such harsh scoffs as
    these.
  Lo! Love, when thou art present, sits at ease,
And bears his mastership so mightily,
That all my troubled senses he thrusts out,
  Sorely tormenting some, and slaying some,
    Till none but he is left and has free range
    To gaze on thee. This makes my face to
      change
  Into another's ; while I stand all dumb,
And hear my senses clamour in their rout.

This sonnet I divide not into parts, because a division is only made to open the meaning of the thing divided: and this, as it is sufficiently manifest through the reasons given, has no need of division. True it is that, amid the words whereby is shown the occasion of this sonnet, dubious words are to be found; namely, when I say that Love kills all my spirits, but that the visual remain in life, only outside of their own instruments. And this difficulty it is impossible for any to solve who is not in equal guise liege unto Love; and, to those who are so, that is manifest which would clear up the dubious words. And therefore it were not well for me to expound this difficulty, inasmuch as my speaking would be either fruitless or else superfluous.

A while after this strange disfigurement, I became possessed with a strong conception which left me but very seldom, and then to return quickly. And it was this: "Seeing that thou comest into such

scorn by the companionship of this lady, wherefore
seekest thou to behold her ? If she should ask thee
this thing, what answer couldst thou make unto
her ? yea, even though thou wert master of all thy
faculties, and in no way hindered from answering."
Unto the which, another very humble thought said
in reply : " If I were master of all my faculties, and
in no way hindered from answering, I would tell
her that no sooner do I image to myself her mar-
vellous beauty than I am possessed with a desire
to behold her, the which is of so great strength that
it kills and destroys in my memory all those things
which might oppose it; and it is therefore that the
great anguish I have endured thereby is yet not
enough to restrain me from seeking to behold her."
And then, because of these thoughts, I resolved to
write somewhat, wherein, having pleaded mine ex-
cuse, I should tell her of what I felt in her presence,
Whereupon I wrote this sonnet :—

THE thoughts are broken in my memory,
   Thou lovely Joy, whene'er I see thy face;
   When thou art near me, Love fills up the space,
Often repeating, " If death irk thee, fly."
My face shows my heart's colour, verily,
   Which, fainting, seeks for any leaning-place;
   Till, in the drunken terror of disgrace,
The very stones seem to be shrieking, "Die!"
It were a grievous sin, if one should not
   Strive then to comfort my bewildered mind
    (Though merely with a simple pitying)
For the great anguish which thy scorn has wrought
   In the dead sight o' the eyes grown nearly blind,
    Which look for death as for a blessed thing.

*This sonnet is divided into two parts. In the first,
I tell the cause why I abstain not from coming to
this lady. In the second, I tell what befalls me
through coming to her; and this part begins here*

5

" When thou art near." And also this second part divides into five distinct statements. For, in the first, I say what Love, counselled by Reason, tells me when I am near the lady. In the second, I set forth the state of my heart by the example of the face. In the third, I say how all ground of trust fails me. In the fourth, I say that he sins who shows not pity of me, which would give me some comfort. In the last, I say why people should take pity: namely, for the piteous look which comes into mine eyes; which piteous look is destroyed, that is, appeareth not unto others, through the jeering of this lady, who draws to the like action those who per-adventure would see this piteousness. The second part begins here, " My face shows; " the third, " Till, in the drunken terror; " the fourth, "It were a grievous sin;" the fifth, "For the great anguish."

Thereafter, this sonnet bred in me desire to write down in verse four other things touching my condition, the which things it seemed to me that I had not yet made manifest. The first among these was the grief that possessed me very often, remembering the strangeness which Love wrought in me; the second was, how Love many times assailed me so suddenly and with such strength that I had no other life remaining except a thought which spake of my lady; the third was, how, when Love did battle with me in this wise, I would rise up all colourless, if so I might see my lady, conceiving that the sight of her would defend me against the assault of Love, and altogether forgetting that which her presence brought unto me; and the fourth was, how, when I saw her, the sight not only defended me not, but took away the little life that remained to me. And I said these four things in a sonnet, which is this :—

AT whiles (yea oftentimes) I muse over
    The quality of anguish that is mine
    Through Love : then pity makes my voice to pine,

Saying, " Is any else thus, anywhere ? "

Love smiteth me, whose strength is ill to bear;

  So that of all my life is left no sign

  Except one thought; and that, because 'tis thine,

Leaves not the body but abideth there.

And then if I, whom other aid forsook,

  Would aid myself, and innocent of art

    Would fain have sight of thee as a last hope,

No sooner do I lift mine eyes to look

    Than the blood seems as shaken from my heart,

    And all my pulses beat at once and stop.

This sonnet is divided into four parts, four things being therein narrated; and as these are set forth above, I only proceed to distinguish the parts by their beginnings. Wherefore I say that the second part begins, "Love smiteth me;" the third, "And then if I;" the fourth, "No sooner do I lift."

After I had written these three last sonnets

wherein I spake unto my lady, telling her almost the whole of my condition, it seemed to me that I should be silent, having said enough concerning myself. But albeit I spake not to her again, yet it behoved me afterward to write of another matter, more noble than the foregoing. And for that the occasion of what I then wrote may be found pleasant in the hearing, I will relate it as briefly as I may.

Through the sore change in mine aspect, the secret of my heart was now understood of many. Which thing being thus, there came a day when certain ladies to whom it was well known (they having been with me at divers times in my trouble) were met together for the pleasure of gentle company. And as I was going that way by chance, (but I think rather by the will of fortune,) I heard one of them call unto me, and she that called was a lady of very sweet speech. And when I had come close up with them, and perceived that they had not among them mine excellent lady, I was reassured; and saluted them, asking of their pleasure The ladies were many; divers of whom were laughing one to another, while divers gazed at me as though I should speak anon. But when I still spake not, one of them, who before had been talking with another, addressed me by my name, saying, "To what end lovest thou this lady, seeing that thou canst not support her presence? Now tell us this thing, that we may know it : for certainly the end of such a love must be worthy of knowledge." And when she had spoken these words, not she only, but all they that were with her, began to observe me, waiting for my reply. Whereupon I said thus unto them :—"Ladies, the end and aim of my Love was but the salutation of that lady of whom I conceive that ye are speaking ; wherein alone I found that beatitude which is the goal of desire. And now that it hath pleased her to deny me this, Love, my Master, of his great goodness, hath placed all my beatitude there where my hope will not fail me." Then those ladies began to talk closely together; and as I have seen snow fall among the rain, so was their talk mingled with sighs. But after a little, that lady who had been the first to address me, addressed me again in these words: "We pray thee that thou wilt tell us wherein abideth this thy beatitude." And answering, I said but thus much: "In those words that do praise my lady." To the which she rejoined: "If thy speech were true, those words that thou didst write concerning thy condition would have been written with another intent."

Then I, being almost put to shame because of her answer, went out from among them; and as I walked, I said within myself: "Seeing that there is so much beatitude in those words which do praise my lady, wherefore hath my speech of her been

different?" And then I resolved that thenceforward
I would choose for the theme of my writings only
the praise of this most gracious being. But when
I had thought exceedingly, it seemed to me that I
had taken to myself a theme which was much too
lofty, so that I dared not begin; and I remained
during several days in the desire of speaking, and
the fear of beginning. After which it happened, as I
passed one day along a path which lay beside a
stream of very clear water, that there came upon me
a great desire to say somewhat in rhyme : but when
I began thinking how I should say it, methought
that to speak of her were unseemly, unless I
spoke to other ladies in the second person ; which
is to say, not to *any* other ladies, but only to such
as are so called because they are gentle, let alone
for mere womanhood. Whereupon I declare that
my tongue spake as though by its own impulse,
and said, "Ladies that have intelligence in love."

These words I laid up in my mind with great glad-
ness, conceiving to take them as my commencement.
Wherefore, having returned to the city I spake of, and
considered thereof during certain days, I began a poem
with this beginning, constructed in the mode which will
be seen below in its division. The poem begins here :—

LADIES that have intelligence in love,
 Of mine own lady I would speak with you ;
 Not that I hope to count her praises through,
  But telling what I may, to ease my mind.
And I declare that when I speak thereof,
Love sheds such perfect sweetness over me
That if my courage failed not, certainly
  To him my listeners must be all resign'd.
  Wherefore I will not speak in such large kind
That mine own speech should foil me, which were
  base ;
But only will discourse of her high grace
  In these poor words, the best that I can find,

With you alone, dear dames and damozels :
Twere ill to speak thereof with any else.

An Angel, of his blessed knowledge, saith
  To God : " Lord, in the world that Thou hast made,
  A miracle in action is display'd,
    By reason of a soul whose splendours fare
Even hither : and since Heaven requireth
Nought saving her, for her it prayeth Thee,
Thy Saints crying aloud continually."
    Yet Pity still defends our earthly share
  In that sweet soul ; God answering thus the prayer :
" My well-belovèd, suffer that in peace
Your hope remain, while so My pleasure is,
  There where one dwells who dreads the loss of her :
And who in Hell unto the doomed shall say,
  I have looked on that for which God's chosen pray.' "

My lady is desired in the high Heaven :
  Wherefore, it now behoveth me to tell,

Saying : Let any maid that would be well

   Esteemed keep with her : for as she goes by,

Into foul hearts a deathly chill is driven

By Love, that makes ill thought to perish there :

While any who endures to gaze on her

   Must either be ennobled, or else die.

   When one deserving to be raised so high

Is found, 'tis then her power attains its proof,

Making his heart strong for his soul's behoof

   With the full strength of meek humility.

Also this virtue owns she, by God's will :

Who speaks with her can never come to ill.

Love saith concerning her : " How chanceth it

   That flesh, which is of dust, should be thus pure ? "

   Then, gazing always, he makes oath : " Forsure,

   This is a creature of God till now unknown."

She hath that paleness of the pearl that's fit

In a fair woman, so much and not more;

She is as high as Nature's skill can soar;
　　Beauty is tried by her comparison.
　　Whatever her sweet eyes are turned upon,
　　Spirits of love do issue thence in flame,
　　Which through their eyes who then may look on them
　　Pierce to the heart's deep chamber every one.
And in her smile Love's image you may see;
Whence none can gaze upon her steadfastly.

Dear Song, I know thou wilt hold gentle speech
　　With many ladies, when I send thee forth:
　　Wherefore (being mindful that thou hadst thy birth
　　From Love, and art a modest, simple child),
Whomso thou meetest, say thou this to each:
" Give me good speed!　To her I wend along
In whose much strength my weakness is made
　　　　strong."
　　　　And if, i' the end, thou wouldst not be beguiled
　　　　Of all thy labour, seek not the defiled

And common sort ; but rather choose to be
Where man and woman dwell in courtesy.

So to the road thou shalt be reconciled,
And find the lady, and with the lady, Love.
Commend thou me to each, as doth behove.

*This poem, that it may be better understood, I will
divide more subtly than the others preceding ; and
therefore I will make three parts of it. The first
part is a proem to the words following. The second
is the matter treated of. The third is, as it were,
a handmaid to the preceding words. The second
begins here, "An Angel ;" the third here, "Dear
Song, I know." The first part is divided into four.
In the first, I say to whom I mean to speak of my
lady, and wherefore I will so speak. In the second,
I say what she appears to myself to be when I reflect
upon her excellence, and what I would utter if I
lost not courage. In the third, I say what it is*

*I purpose to speak so as not to be impeded by
faintheartedness. In the fourth, repeating to whom
I purpose speaking, I tell the reason why I speak
to them. The second begins here, "And I declare;"
the third here, "Wherefore I will not speak;" the
fourth here, "With you alone." Then, when I say
"An Angel," I begin treating of this lady: and
this part is divided into two. In the first, I tell
what is understood of her in heaven. In the second,
I tell what is understood of her on earth: here, "My
lady is desired." This second part is divided into
two; for, in the first, I speak of her as regards the
nobleness of her soul, relating some of her virtues
proceeding from her soul; in the second, I speak of
her as regards the nobleness of her body, narrating
some of her beauties: here, "Love saith concerning
her." This second part is divided into two, for,
in the first, I speak of certain beauties which belong
to the whole person; in the second, I speak of certain*

beauties which belong to a distinct part of the person:
here, "*Whatever her sweet eyes.*" This second part
is divided into two; for, in the one, I speak of the
eyes, which are the beginning of love; in the second,
I speak of the mouth, which is the end of love. And
that every vicious thought may be discarded here-
from, let the reader remember that it is above written
that the greeting of this lady, which was an act of
her mouth, was the goal of my desires, while I
could receive it. Then, when I say, "*Dear Song,
I know,*" I add a stanza as it were handmaid to the
others, wherein I say what I desire from this my
poem. And because this last part is easy to under-
stand, I trouble not myself with more divisions. I
say, indeed, that the further to open the meaning of
this poem, more minute divisions ought to be used;
but nevertheless he who is not of wit enough to
understand it by these which have been already made
is welcome to leave it alone; for certes, I fear 1

*have communicated its sense to too many by these present
divisions, if it so happened that many should hear it.*

When this song was a little gone abroad, a certain
one of my friends, hearing the same, was pleased to
question me, that I should tell him what thing love
is; it may be, conceiving from the words thus heard a
hope of me beyond my desert. Wherefore I, thinking
that after such discourse it were well to say some-
what of the nature of Love, and also in accordance
with my friend's desire, proposed to myself to write
certain words in the which I should treat of this argu-
ment. And the sonnet that I then made is this:—

Love and the gentle heart are one same thing,
    Even as the wise man* in his ditty saith:
    Each, of itself, would be such life in death
As rational soul bereft of reasoning.

* Guido Guinicelli, in the canzone which begins, "Within
the gentle heart Love shelters him."

'Tis Nature makes them when she loves : a king
 Love is, whose palace where he sojourneth
 Is called the Heart; there draws he quiet breath
At first, with brief or longer slumbering.
Then beauty seen in virtuous womankind
 Will make the eyes desire, and through the heart
 Send the desiring of the eyes again;
Where often it abides so long enshrin'd
 That Love at length out of his sleep will start.
 And women feel the same for worthy men.

This sonnet is divided into two parts. In the first, I speak of him according to his power. In the second, I speak of him according as his power translates itself into act. The second part begins here, " Then beauty seen." The first is divided into two. In the first, I say in what subject this power exists. In the second, I say how this subject and this power are produced together, and how the

6

one regards the other, as form does matter. The second begins here, "'Tis Nature." Afterwards when I say, "Then beauty seen in virtuous womankind," I say how this power translates itself into act; and, first, how it so translates itself in a man, then how it so translates itself in a woman: here, "And women feel."

Having treated of love in the foregoing, it appeared to me that I should also say something in praise of my lady, wherein it might be set forth how love manifested itself when produced by her; and how not only she could awaken it where it slept, but where it was not she could marvellously create it. To the which end I wrote another sonnet; and it is this :—

My lady carries love within her eyes;

　All that she looks on is made pleasanter;

　Upon her path men turn to gaze at her;

　He whom she greeteth feels his heart to rise,

And droops his troubled visage, full of sighs,
    And of his evil heart is then aware:
    Hate loves, and pride becomes a worshipper.
O women, help to praise her in somewise.
Humbleness, and the hope that hopeth well,
    By speech of hers into the mind are brought,
    And who beholds is blessèd oftenwhiles.
    The look she hath when she a little smiles
    Cannot be said, nor holden in the thought;
'Tis such a new and gracious miracle.

This sonnet has three sections. In the first, I say how this lady brings this power into action by those most noble features, her eyes; and, in the third, I say this same as to that most noble feature, her mouth. And between these two sections is a little section, which asks, as it were, help for the previous section and the subsequent; and it begins here, "O women, help." The third begins

here, "Humbleness." The first is divided into
three; for, in the first, I say how she with power
makes noble that which she looks upon; and this
is as much as to say that she brings Love, in
power, thither where he is not. In the second, I
say how she brings Love, in act, into the hearts
of all those whom she sees. In the third, I tell
what she afterwards, with virtue, operates upon
their hearts. The second begins, "Upon her path;"
the third, "He whom she greeteth." Then, when
I say, "O women, help," I intimate to whom it is
my intention to speak, calling on women to help
me to honour her. Then, when I say, "Humble-
ness," I say that same which is said in the first
part, regarding two acts of her mouth, one whereof
is her most sweet speech, and the other her
marvellous smile. Only, I say not of this last
how it operates upon the hearts of others, because
memory cannot retain this smile, nor its operation.

Not many days after this (it being the will of the most High God, who also from Himself put not away death), the father of wonderful Beatrice, going out of this life, passed certainly into glory. Thereby it happened, as of very sooth it might not be other- wise, that this lady was made full of the bitterness of grief: seeing that such a parting is very grievous unto those friends who are left, and that no other friendship is like to that between a good parent and a good child; and furthermore considering that this lady was good in the supreme degree, and her father (as by many it hath been truly averred) of exceeding goodness. And because it is the usage of that city that men meet with men in such a grief, and women with women, certain ladies of her com- panionship gathered themselves unto Beatrice, where she kept alone in her weeping: and as they passed in and out, I could hear them speak concerning her, how she wept. At length two of them went by me, who said: "Certainly she grieveth in such sort that one might die for pity, beholding her." Then, feeling the tears upon my face, I put up my hands to hide them: and had it not been that I hoped to hear more concerning her (seeing that where I sat, her friends passed continually in and out), I should assuredly have gone thence to be alone, when I felt the tears come. But as I still sat in that place, certain ladies again passed near me, who were saying among themselves: "Which of us shall be joyful any more, who have listened to this lady in her piteous sorrow?" And there were others who said as they went by me: "He that sitteth here could not weep more if he had beheld her as we have beheld her;" and again: "He is so altered that he seemeth not as himself." And still as the ladies passed to and fro, I could hear them speak after this fashion of her and of me.

Wherefore afterwards, having considered and perceiving that there was herein matter for poesy, I resolved that I would write certain rhymes in the which should be contained all that those ladies had said. And because I would willingly have spoken to them if it had not been for discreetness, I made in my rhymes as though I had spoken and they had answered me. And thereof I wrote two sonnets; in the first of which I addressed them as I would fain have done; and in the second related their answer, using the speech that I had heard from them, as though it had been spoken unto myself. And the sonnets are these :—

I.

You that thus wear a modest countenance
  With lids weigh'd down by the heart's heaviness,
  Whence come you, that among you every face
Appears the same, for its pale troubled glance?
Have you beheld my lady's face, perchance,

Bow'd with the grief that Love makes full of grace ?

Say now, " This thing is thus ; " as my heart says,

Marking your grave and sorrowful advance.

And if indeed you come from where she sighs

   And mourns, may it please you (for his heart's relief)

     To tell how it fares with her unto him

Who knows that you have wept, seeing your eyes,

   And is so grieved with looking on your grief

     That his heart trembles and his sight grows dim.

This sonnet is divided into two parts. In the first, I call and ask these ladies whether they come from her, telling them that I think they do, because they return the nobler. In the second, I pray them to tell me of her; and the second begins here, " And if indeed."

II.

CANST thou indeed be he that still would sing

   Of our dear lady unto none but us ?

For though thy voice confirms that it is thus,
Thy visage might another witness bring.
And wherefore is thy grief so sore a thing
   That grieving thou mak'st others dolorous?
   Hast thou too seen her weep, that thou from us
Canst not conceal thine inward sorrowing?
Nay, leave our woe to us: let us alo:
   'Twere sin if one should strive to soothe our woe,
     For in her weeping we have heard her speak:
Also her look's so full of her heart's moan
   That they who should behold her, looking so,
     Must fall aswoon, feeling all life grow weak.

This sonnet has four parts, as the ladies in whose person I reply had four forms of answer. And, because these are sufficiently shown above, I stay not to explain the purport of the parts, and therefore I only discriminate them. The second begins here, "And wherefore is thy grief;" the third here,

"*Nay, leave our woe;*" *the fourth,* "*Also her look.*"

A few days after this, my body became afflicted with a painful infirmity, whereby I suffered bitter anguish for many days, which at last brought me unto such weakness that I could no longer move. And I remember that on the ninth day, being over-come with intolerable pain, a thought came into my mind concerning my lady : but when it had a little nourished this thought, my mind returned to its brooding over mine enfeebled body. And then perceiving.how frail a thing life is, even though health keep with it, the matter seemed to me so pitiful that I could not choose but weep ; and weeping I said within myself : "Certainly it must some time come to pass that the very gentle Beatrice will die." Then, feeling bewildered, I closed mine eyes ; and my brain began to be in travail as the brain of one frantic, and to have such imaginations as here follow.

And at the first, it seemed to me that I saw certain faces of women with their hair loosened, which called out to me, " Thou shalt surely die ; " after the which, other terrible and unknown appearances said unto me, " Thou art dead." At length, as my phantasy held on in its wanderings, I came to be I knew not where, and to behold a throng of dishevelled ladies wonderfully sad, who kept going hither and thither weeping. Then the sun went out, so that the stars showed themselves, and they were of such a colour that I knew they must be weeping : and it seemed to me that the birds fell dead out of the sky, and that there were great earthquakes. With that, while I wondered in my trance, and was filled with a grievous fear, I conceived that a certain friend came unto me and said : " Hast thou not heard ? She that was thine excellent lady hath been taken out of life." Then I began to weep very piteously ; and not only in mine imagination, but with mine eyes, which were wet with tears. And I seemed to look towards Heaven, and to behold a multitude of angels who were returning upwards, having before them an exceedingly white cloud : and these angels were singing together gloriously, and the words of their song were these : " *Osanna in excelsis* ; " and there was no more that I heard. Then my heart that was so full of love said unto me : " It is true that our lady lieth dead ; " and it seemed to me that I went to look upon the body wherein that blessed and most noble spirit had had its abiding-place. And so strong was this idle imagining, that it made me to behold my lady in death ; whose head certain ladies seemed to be covering with a white veil ; and who was so humble of her aspect that it was as though she had said, " I have attained to look on the beginning of peace." And therewithal I came unto such humility by the sight of her, that I cried out upon Death, saying : " Now come unto me, and

be not bitter against me any longer: surely, there
where thou hast been, thou hast learned gentleness.
Wherefore come now unto me who do greatly desire
thee: seest thou not that I wear thy colour already?"
And when I had seen all those offices performed
that are fitting to be done unto the dead, it seemed
to me that I went back unto mine own chamber,
and looked up towards Heaven. And so strong
was my phantasy, that I wept again in very truth,
and said with my true voice: "O excellent soul!
how blessed is he that now looketh upon thee!"

And as I said these words, with a painful anguish
of sobbing and another prayer unto Death, a young
and gentle lady, who had been standing beside me
where I lay, conceiving that I wept and cried out
because of the pain of mine infirmity, was taken
with trembling and began to shed tears. Whereby
other ladies, who were about the room, becoming
aware of my discomfort by reason of the moan that

she made, (who indeed was of my very near kindred,) led her away from where I was, and then set themselves to awaken me, thinking that I dreamed, and saying: "Sleep no longer, and be not disquieted."

Then, by their words, this strong imagination was brought suddenly to an end, at the moment that I was about to say, " O Beatrice! peace be with thee." And already I had said, "O Beatrice!" when being aroused, I opened mine eyes, and knew that it had been a deception. But albeit I had indeed uttered her name, yet my voice was so broken with sobs, that it was not understood by these ladies; so that in spite of the sore shame that I felt, I turned towards them by Love's counselling. And when they beheld me, they began to say, "He seemeth as one dead," and to whisper among themselves, " Let us strive if we may not comfort him." Whereupon they spake to me many soothing words, and questioned me moreover touching the cause of my

fear. Then I, being somewhat reassured, and having
perceived that it was a mere phantasy, said unto
them, "This thing it was that made me afeard;"
and told them of all that I had seen, from the be-
ginning even unto the end, but without once speaking
the name of my lady. Also, after I had recovered
from my sickness, I bethought me to write these
things in rhyme; deeming it a lovely thing to be
known. Whereof I wrote this poem :—

A VERY pitiful lady, very young,
  Exceeding rich in human sympathies,
    Stood by, what time I clamour'd upon Death;
And at the wild words wandering on my tongue
  And at the piteous look within mine eyes
    She was affrighted, that sobs choked her breath.
    So by her weeping where I lay beneath,
Some other gentle ladies came to know
My state, and made her go :

Afterward, bending themselves over me,

One said, "Awaken thee!"

And one, "What thing thy sleep disquieteth?"

With that, my soul woke up from its eclipse,

The while my lady's name rose to my lips:

But utter'd in a voice so sob-broken,

So feeble with the agony of tears,

That I alone might hear it in my heart;

And though that look was on my visage then

Which he who is ashamed so plainly wears,

Love made that I through shame held not apart,

But gazed upon them. And my hue was such

That they look'd at each other and thought of death;

Saying under their breath

Most tenderly, "O let us comfort him:"

Then unto me: "What dream

Was thine, that it hath shaken thee so much?"

And when I was a little comforted,

"This, ladies, was the dream I dreamt," I said.

"I was a-thinking how life fails with us
  Suddenly after such a little while;
    When Love sobb'd in my heart, which is his home
Whereby my spirit wax'd so dolorous
  That in myself I said, with sick recoil:
    'Yea, to my lady too this Death must come.'
    And therewithal such a bewilderment
Possess'd me, that I shut mine eyes for peace;
And in my brain did cease
  Order of thought, and every healthful thing.
  Afterwards, wandering
    Amid a swarm of doubts that came and went,
Some certain women's faces hurried by,
And shriek'd to me, 'Thou too shalt die, shalt die!'

"Then saw I many broken hinted sights
  In the uncertain state I stepp'd into.
    Meseem'd to be I know not in what place,
Where ladies through the street, like mournful lights,

Ran with loose hair, and eyes that frighten'd you
  By their own terror, and a pale amaze :
  The while, little by little, as I thought,
The sun ceased, and the stars began to gather,
And each wept at the other ;
  And birds dropp'd in mid-flight out of the sky ;
  And earth shook suddenly ;
  And I was 'ware of one, hoarse and tired out,
Who ask'd of me : 'Hast thou not heard it said ?...
Thy lady, she that was so fair, is dead.'

'Then lifting up mine eyes, as the tears came,
  I saw the Angels, like a rain of manna,
  In a long flight flying back Heavenward ;
Having a little cloud in front of them,
  After the which they went and said, 'Hosanna ; '
  And if they had said more, you should have heard.
  Then Love said, 'Now shall all things be made
    clear :

Come and behold our lady where she lies.
These 'wildering phantasies
    Then carried me to see my lady dead.
    Even as I there was led,
        Her ladies with a veil were covering her;
And with her was such very humbleness
That she appeared to say, 'I am at peace.'

"And I became so humble in my grief,
    Seeing in her such deep humility,
        That I said: 'Death, I hold thee passing good
Henceforth, and a most gentle sweet relief,
    Since my dear love has chosen to dwell with
        thee:
    Pity, not hate, is thine, well understood.
    Lo! I do so desire to see thy face
That I am like as one who nears the tomb;
My soul entreats thee, Come.'
    Then I departed, having made my moan;

And when I was alone

    I said, and cast my eyes to the High Place:

'Blessed is he, fair soul, who meets thy glance!'

. . . . . . Just then you woke me, of your

    complaisaùnce."

This poem has two parts. In the first, speaking to a person undefined, I tell how I was aroused from a vain phantasy by certain ladies, and how I promised them to tell what it was. In the second, I say how I told them. The second part begins here, "I was a-thinking." The first part divides into two. In the first, I tell that which certain ladies, and which one singly, did and said because of my phantasy, before I had returned into my right senses. In the second, I tell what these ladies said to me after I had left off this wandering: and it begins here, "But uttered in a voice." Then, when I say, "I was a-thinking," I say how I told them this

*my imagination; and concerning this I have two
parts. In the first, I tell, in order, this imagination.
In the second, saying at what time they called me,
I covertly thank them: and this part begins here,
"Just then you woke me."*

After this empty imagining, it happened on a day,
as I sat thoughtful, that I was taken with such a
strong trembling at the heart, that it could not have
been otherwise in the presence of my lady. Where-
upon I perceived that there was an appearance of
Love beside me, and I seemed to see him coming
from my lady; and he said, not aloud but within
my heart: "Now take heed that thou bless the day
when I entered into thee; for it is fitting that thou
shouldst do so." And with that my heart was so
full of gladness, that I could hardly believe it to be
of very truth mine own heart and not another.

A short while after these words which my heart
spoke to me with the tongue of Love, I saw coming

towards me a certain lady who was very famous for her beauty, and of whom that friend whom I have already called the first among my friends had long been enamoured. This lady's right name was Joan; but because of her comeliness (or at least it was so imagined) she was called of many *Primavera* (Spring), and went by that name among them. Then looking again, I perceived that the most noble Beatrice followed after her. And when both these ladies had passed by me, it seemed to me that Love spake again in my heart, saying: "She that came first was called Spring, only because of that which was to happen on this day. And it was I myself who caused that name to be given her; seeing that as the Spring cometh first in the year, so should she come first on this day,* when Beatrice was to show

* There is a play in the original upon the words *Primavera* (Spring) and *prima verrà* (she shall come first), to which I have given as near an equivalent as I could.

herself after the vision of her servant. And even if thou go about to consider her right name, it is also as one should say, 'She shall come first;' inasmuch as her name, Joan, is taken from that John who went before the True Light, saying: '*Ego vox clamantis in deserto: Parate viam Domini.*'"* And also it seemed to me that he added other words, to wit: "He who should inquire delicately touching this matter, could not but call Beatrice by mine own name, which is to say, Love; beholding her so like unto me."

Then I, having thought of this, imagined to write it with rhymes and send it unto my chief friend; but setting aside certain words † which seemed

---

* "I am the voice of one crying in the wilderness: 'Prepare ye the way of the Lord.'"

† That is (as I understand it), suppressing, from delicacy towards his friend, the words in which Love describes Joan as merely the forerunner of Beatrice. And perhaps in the

proper to be set aside, because I believed that his heart still regarded the beauty of her that was called Spring. And I wrote this sonnet :—

I FELT a spirit of love begin to stir
    Within my heart, long time unfelt till then ;
    And saw Love coming towards me, fair and fain
(That I scarce knew him for his joyful cheer),
Saying, " Be now indeed my worshipper ! "
    And in his speech he laugh'd and laugh'd again.
    Then, while it was his pleasure to remain,
I chanced to look the way he had drawn near,
And saw the Ladies Joan and Beatrice
    Approach me, this the other following,
    One and a second marvel instantly.

latter part of this sentence a reproach is gently conveyed to the fickle Guido Cavalcanti, who may already have transferred his homage (though Dante had not then learned it) from Joan to Mandetta.

And even as now my memory speaketh this,
  Love spake it then : " The first is christen'd
    Spring ;
  The second Love, she is so like to me."

*This sonnet has many parts : whereof the first
tells how I felt awakened within my heart the
accustomed tremor, and how it seemed that Love
appeared to me joyful from afar. The second says
how it appeared to me that Love spake within my
heart, and what was his aspect. The third tells
how, after he had in such wise been with me a space,
I saw and heard certain things. The second part
begins here, "Saying, ' Be now ; ' " the third here,
" Then, while it was his pleasure." The third part
divides into two. In the first, I say what I saw.
In the second, I say what I heard ; and it begins
here, " Love spake it then."*

It might be here objected unto me, (and even

by one worthy of controversy,) that I have spoken
ot Love as though it were a thing outward and
visible: not only a spiritual essence, but as a
bodily substance also. The which thing, in absolute
truth, is a fallacy; Love not being of itself a
substance, but an accident of substance. Yet that
I speak of Love as though it were a thing
tangible and even human, appears by three things
which I say thereof. And firstly, I say that I
perceived Love coming towards me; whereby,
seeing that *to come* bespeaks locomotion, and
seeing also how philosophy teacheth us that none
but a corporeal substance hath locomotion, it
seemeth that I speak ot Love as of a corporeal
substance. And secondly, I say that Love smiled :
and thirdly, that Love spake; faculties (and
especially the risible faculty) which appear proper
unto man: whereby it further seemeth that I
speak of Love as of a man. Now that this

matter may be explained (as is fitting), it must first be remembered that anciently they who wrote poems of Love wrote not in the vulgar tongue, but rather certain poets in the Latin tongue. I mean, among us, although perchance the same may have been among others, and although likewise, as among the Greeks, they were not writers of spoken language, but men of letters, treated of these things.* And indeed it is not a great number of years since poetry

---

* On reading Dante's treatise *De Vulgari Eloquio*, it will be found that the distinction which he intends here is not between one language, or dialect, and another; but between "vulgar speech" (that is, the language handed down from mother to son without any conscious use of grammar or syntax), and language as regulated by grammarians and the laws of literary composition, and which Dante calls simply "Grammar." A great deal might be said on the bearings of the present passage, but it is no part of my plan to enter on such questions.

began to be made in the vulgar tongue; the writing of rhymes in spoken language corresponding to the writing in metre of Latin verse, by a certain analogy. And I say that it is but a little while, because if we examine the language of *oco* and the language of *sì*,* we shall not find in those tongues any written thing of an earlier date than the last hundred and fifty years. Also the reason why certain of a very mean sort obtained at the first some fame as poets is, that before them no man had written verses in the language of *sì:* and of these, the first was moved to the writing of such verses by the wish to make himself understood of a certain lady, unto whom Latin poetry was difficult. This thing is against such as rhyme concerning other matters than love; that mode of speech having been first used for

---

* *i.e.*, the languages of Provence and Tuscany.

the expression of love alone.* Wherefore, seeing that poets have a license allowed them that is not allowed unto the writers of prose, and seeing also that they who write in rhyme are simply poets in the vulgar tongue, it becomes fitting and reasonable that a larger license should be given to these than to other modern writers; and that any metaphor or rhetorical similitude which is permitted unto poets, should also be counted not

---

* It strikes me that this curious passage furnishes a reason, hitherto (I believe) overlooked, why Dante put such of his lyrical poems as relate to philosophy into the form of love-poems. He liked writing in Italian rhyme rather than Latin metre; he thought Italian rhyme ought to be confined to love-poems: therefore whatever he wrote (at this age) had to take the form of a love-poem. Thus any poem by Dante not concerning love is later than his twenty-seventh year (1291-2), when he wrote the prose of the *Vita Nuova* ; the poetry having been written earlier, at the time of the events referred to.

unseemly in the rhymers of the vulgar tongue. Thus, if we perceive that the former have caused inanimate things to speak as though they had sense and reason, and to discourse one with another; yea, and not only actual things, but such also as have no real existence, (seeing that they have made things which are not, to speak; and oftentimes written of those which are merely accidents as though they were substances and things hûman); it should therefore be permitted to the latter to do the like; which is to say, not inconsiderately, but with such sufficient motive as may afterwards be set forth in prose.

That the Latin poets have done thus, appears through Virgil, where he saith that Juno (to wit, a goddess hostile to the Trojans) spake unto Æolus, master of the Winds; as it is written in the first book of the Æneid, *Æole, namque tibi, etc.;* and that this master of the Winds made reply : *Tuus, o regina, quid optes—Explorare labor, mihi iussa capessere fas est.* And through the same poet, the inanimate thing speaketh unto the animate, in the third book of the Æneid, where it is written: *Dardanidæ duri, etc.* With Lucan, the animate thing speaketh to the inanimate; as thus: *Multum, Roma, tamen debes civilibus armis.* In Horace, man is made to speak to his own intelligence as unto another person ; (and not only hath Horace done this, but herein he followeth the excellent Homer), as thus in his Poetics: *Dic mihi, Musa, virum, etc.* Through Ovid, Love speaketh as a human creature, in the beginning of his discourse *De Remediis Amoris:* as thus: *Bella mihi, video, bella parantur, ait.* By which ensamples this thing shall be made manifest unto such as may be offended at any part of this my book. And lest some of the common sort should be moved to jeering hereat, I will here add, that neither did these ancient poets speak thus without consideration, nor should they who are makers of rhyme in our day write after the same fashion, having no reason in what they write; for it were a shameful thing if one should rhyme under the semblance of metaphor or rhetorical similitude, and afterwards, being questioned thereof, should be unable to rid his words of such semblance, unto their right understanding. Of whom, (to wit, of such as rhyme thus foolishly,) myself and the first among my friends do know many.

But returning to the matter of my discourse. This excellent lady, of whom I spake in what hath gone before, came at last into such favour with all men, that when she passed anywhere folk ran to behold her; which thing was a deep joy to me: and when she drew near unto any, so much truth and simpleness entered into his heart, that he dared neither to lift his eyes nor to return her salutation:

and unto this, many who have felt it can bear witness. She went along crowned and clothed with humility, showing no whit of pride in all that she heard and saw: and when she had gone by, it was said of many, "This is not a woman, but one of the beautiful angels of Heaven:" and there were some that said: "This is surely a miracle; blessed be the Lord, who hath power to work thus marvellously." I say, of very sooth, that she showed herself so gentle and so full of all perfection, that she bred in those who looked upon her a soothing quiet beyond any speech; neither could any look upon her without sighing immediately. These things, and things yet more wonderful, were brought to pass through her miraculous virtue. Wherefore I, considering thereof and wishing to resume the endless tale of her praises, resolved to write somewhat wherein I might dwell on her surpassing influence; to the end that

8

not only they who had beheld her, but others also,
might know as much concerning her as words could
give to the understanding. And it was then that I
wrote this sonnet :—

My lady looks so gentle and so pure

   When yielding salutat on by the way,

   That the tongue trembles and has nought to say,

And the eyes, which fain would see, may not endure.

And still, amid the praise she hears secure,

   She walks with humbleness for her array ;

   Seeming a creature sent from Heaven to stay

On earth, and show a miracle made sure.

She is so pleasant in the eyes of men

That through the sight the inmost heart doth gain

   A sweetness which needs proof to know it by :

And from between her lips there seems to move

A soothing essence that is full of love,

   Saying for ever to the spirit, " Sigh ! "

This sonnet is so easy to understand, from what is afore narrated, that it needs no division; and therefore, leaving it, I say also that this excellent lady came into such favour with all men, that not only she herself was honoured and commended, but through her companionship, honour and commendation came unto others. Wherefore I, perceiving this, and wishing that it should also be made manifest to those that beheld it not, wrote the sonnet here following; wherein is signified the power which her virtue had upon other ladies :—

FOR certain he hath seen all perfectness
   Who among other ladies hath seen mine :
   They that go with her humbly should combine
To thank their God for such peculiar grace
So perfect is the beauty of her face
   That it begets in no wise any sign
   Of envy, but draws round her a clear line

Of love, and blessed faith, and gentleness.

Merely the sight of her makes all things bow:

  Not she herself alone is holier

    Than all; but hers, through her, are raised above.

From all her acts such lovely graces flow

  That truly one may never think of her

    Without a passion of exceeding love.

This sonnet has three parts. In the first, I say in what company this lady appeared most wondrous. In the second, I say how gracious was her society. In the third, I tell of the things which she, with power, worked upon others. The second begins here, "They that go with her;" the third here, "So perfect." This last part divides into three. In the first, I tell what she operated upon women, that is, by their own faculties. In the second, I tell what she operated in them through others. In the third, I say how she not only operated in women, but in

all people; and not only while herself present, but,
by memory of her, operated wondrously. The second
begins here, "Merely the sight;" the third here,
"From all her acts."

Thereafter on a day, I began to consider that
which I had said of my lady : to wit, in these two
sonnets aforegone : and becoming aware that I had
not spoken of her immediate effect on me at that
especial time, it seemed to me that I had spoken
defectively. Whereupon I resolved to write some-
what of the manner wherein I was then subject
to her influence, and of what her influence then
was. And conceiving that I should not be able to
say these things in the small compass of a sonnet,
I began therefore a poem with this beginning :—

LOVE hath so long possessed me for his own
   And made his lordship so familiar
That he, who at first irked me, is now grown

Unto my heart as its best secrets are.

And thus, when he in such sore wise doth mar
My life that all its strength seems gone from it,
Mine inmost being then feels throughly quit
Of anguish, and all evil keeps afar.
Love also gathers to such power in me
That my sighs speak, each one a grievous thing,
Always soliciting
My lady's salutation piteously.
Whenever she beholds me, it is so,
Who is more sweet than any words can show.

   *   *   *   *   *   *

   *   *   *   *   *   *

Quomodo sedet sola civitas plena populo! facta est quasi vidua domina gentium ! *

I was still occupied with this poem, (having

* " How doth the city sit solitary, that was full of people ! how is she become as a widow, she that was great among the nations !"—*Lamentations of Jeremiah*, i. 1.

composed thereof only the above-written stanza,)
when the Lord God of justice called my most
gracious lady unto Himself, that she might be
glorious under the banner of that blessed Queen
Mary, whose name had always a deep reverence in
the words of holy Beatrice. And because haply it
might be found good that I should say somewhat
concerning her departure, I will herein declare
what are the reasons which make that I shall not
do so.

And the reasons are three. The first is, that
such matter belongeth not of right to the present
argument, if one consider the opening of this
little book. The second is, that even though the
present argument required it, my pen doth not
suffice to write in a fit manner of this thing. And the
third is, that were it both possible and of absolute
necessity, it would still be unseemly for me to
speak thereof, seeing that thereby it must behove

me to speak also mine own praises : a thing that
in whosoever doeth it is worthy of blame. For the
which reasons, I will leave this matter to be treated
of by some other than myself.

Nevertheless, as the number nine, which number
hath often had mention in what hath gone before,
(and not, as it might appear, without reason,) seems
also to have borne a part in the manner of her
death: it is therefore right that I should say
somewhat thereof. And for this cause, having first
said what was the part it bore herein, I will after-
wards point out a reason which made that this
number was so closely allied unto my lady.

I say, then, that according to the division of time
in Italy, her most noble spirit departed from among
us in the first hour of the ninth day of the month;
and according to the division of time in Syria, in
the ninth month of the year: seeing that Tismim,
which with us is October, is there the first month.

Also she was taken from among us in that year of our reckoning (to wit, of the years of our Lord) in which the perfect number was nine times multiplied within that century wherein she was born into the world: which is to say, the thirteenth century of Christians.*

And touching the reason why this number was so closely allied unto her, it may peradventure be this. According to Ptolemy (and also to the Christian verity), the revolving heavens are nine; and according to the common opinion among astrologers, these nine heavens together have influence over the

---

* Beatrice Portinari will thus be found to have died during the first hour of the 9th of June, 1290. And from what Dante says at the commencement of this work, (viz., that she was younger than himself by eight or nine months,) it may also be gathered that her age, at the time of her death, was twenty-four years and three months. The "perfect number" mentioned in the present passage is the number ten.

earth. Wherefore it would appear that this number was thus allied unto her for the purpose of signifying that, at her birth, all these nine heavens were at perfect unity with each other as to their influence. This is one reason that may be brought: but more narrowly considering, and according to the infallible truth, this number was her own self: that is to say, by similitude. As thus. The number three is the root of the number nine; seeing that without the interposition of any other number, being multiplied merely by itself, it produceth nine, as we manifestly perceive that three times three are nine. Thus, three being of itself the efficient of nine, and the Great Efficient of Miracles being of Himself Three Persons (to wit: the Father, the Son, and the Holy Spirit), which, being Three, are also One:— this lady was accompanied by the number nine to the end that men might clearly perceive her to be a nine, that is, a miracle, whose only root is the

Holy Trinity. It may be that a more subtile person would find for this thing a reason of greater subtilty : but such is the reason that I find, and that liketh me best.

After this most gracious creature had gone out from among us, the whole city came to be as it were widowed and despoiled of all dignity. Then I, left mourning in this desolate city, wrote unto the principal persons thereof, in an epistle, concerning its condition; taking for my commencement those words of Jeremias: *Quomodo sedet sola civitas! etc.* And I make mention of this, that none may marvel wherefore I set down these words before, in beginning to treat of her death. Also if any should blame me, in that I do not transcribe that epistle whereof I have spoken, I will make it mine excuse that I began this little book with the intent that it should be written altogether in the vulgar tongue; wherefore, seeing that the epistle I speak of is in Latin, it belongeth not to mine undertaking: more especially as I know that my chief friend, for whom I write this book, wished also that the whole of it should be in the vulgar tongue.

When mine eyes had wept for some while, until they were so weary with weeping that I could no longer through them give ease to my sorrow, I bethought me that a few mournful words might stand me instead of tears. And therefore I proposed to make a poem, that weeping I might speak therein of he for whom so much sorrow had destroyed my spirit; and I then began "The eyes that weep."

That this poem may seem to remain the more widowed at its close, I will divide it before writing it; and this method I will observe henceforward. I say that this poor little poem has three parts. The first is a prelude. In the second, I speak of her. In the third, I speak pitifully to the poem. The second begins here, "Beatrice is gone up;" the third here, "Weep, pitiful Song of mine." The first divides into three. In the first, I say what moves me to speak. In the second, I say to whom I mean to speak. In the third, I say of whom I mean to speak. The second begins here, "And because often, thinking;" the third here, "And I will say." Then, when I say, "Beatrice is gone up," I speak of her; and concerning this I have two parts. First, I tell the cause why she was taken away from us: afterwards, I say how one weeps her parting; and this part commences here, "Wonderfully." This part divides into three. In the first, I say who it is that weeps her not. In the second, I say who it is that doth weep her. In the third, I speak of my condition. The second begins here, "But sighing comes, and grief;" the third, "With sighs." Then, when I say, "Weep, pitiful Song of mine," I speak to this my song, telling it what ladies to go to, and stay with.

THE eyes that weep for pity of the heart

   Have wept so long that their grief languisheth,

     And they have no more tears to weep withal :

And now, if I would ease me of a part

   Of what, little by little, leads to death,

     It must be done by speech, or not at all.

     And because often, thinking, I recall

How it was pleasant, ere she went afar,

   To talk of her with you, kind damozels,

   I talk with no one else,

But only with such hearts as women's are.

   And I will say,—still sobbing as speech fails,—

That she hath gone to Heaven suddenly,

And hath left Love below, to mourn with me.

Beatrice is gone up into high Heaven,

   The kingdom where the angels are at peace ;

     And lives with them ; and to her friends is

       dead.

Not by the frost of winter was she driven
  Away, like others; nor by summer-heats;
    But through a perfect gentleness, instead.
    For from the lamp of her meek lowlihead
Such an exceeding glory went up hence
  That it woke wonder in the Eternal Sire,
  Until a sweet desire
Entered Him for that lovely excellence,
  So that He bade her to Himself aspire;
Counting this weary and most evil place
Unworthy of a thing so full of grace.

Wonderfully out of the beautiful form
  Soared her clear spirit, waxing glad the while;
    And is in its first home, there where it is.
Who speaks thereof, and feels not the tears warm
  Upon his face, must have become so vile
    As to be dead to all sweet sympathies.
    Out upon him! an abject wretch like this

May not imagine anything of her,—

    He needs no bitter tears for his relief.

    But sighing comes, and grief,

And the desire to find no comforter,

    (Save only Death, who makes all sorrow

        brief),

To him who for a while turns in his thought

How she hath been among us, and is not.

With sighs my bosom always laboureth

    In thinking, as I do continually,

        Of her for whom my heart now breaks apace;

And very often when I think of death,

    Such a great inward longing comes to me

        That it will change the colour of my face;

        And, if the idea settles in its place,

All my limbs shake as with an ague-fit:

    Till, starting up in wild bewilderment,

    I do become so shent

That I go forth, lest folk misdoubt of it.

   Afterward, calling with a sore lament

On Beatrice, I ask, " Canst thou be dead ? "

And calling on her, I am comforted.

Grief with its tears, and anguish with its sighs,

   Come to me now whene'er I am alone;

      So that I think the sight of me gives pain.

And what my life hath been, that living dies,

   Since for my lady the New Birth's begun,

      I have not any language to explain.

      And so, dear ladies, though my heart were fain,

I scarce could tell indeed how I am thus.

   All joy is with my bitter life at war ;

   Yea, I am fallen so far

That all men seem to say, " Go out from us, "

   Eyeing my cold white lips, how dead they are.

But she, though I be bowed unto the dust,

Watches me ; and will guerdon me, I trust.

                 9

Weep, pitiful Song of mine, upon thy way,
    To the dames going and the damozels
    For whom and for none else
Thy sisters have made music many a day.
Thou, that art very sad and not as they,
    Go dwell thou with them as a mourner dwells.

After I had written this poem, I received the visit of a friend whom I counted as second unto me in the degrees of friendship, and who, moreover, had been united by the nearest kindred to that most gracious creature. And when we had a little spoken together, he began to solicit me that I would write somewhat in memory of a lady who had died; and he disguised his speech, so as to seem to be speaking of another who was but lately dead: wherefore I, perceiving that his speech was of none other than that blessed one herself, told him that it should be done as he required. Then afterwards, having thought thereof, I imagined to give vent in a sonnet to some part of my hidden lamentations; but in such sort that it might seem to be spoken by this friend of mine, to whom I was to give it. And the sonnet saith thus: "Stay now with me," etc.

This sonnet has two parts. In the first, I call the Faithful of Love to hear me. In the second, I relate my miserable condition. The second begins here, "Mark how they force."

STAY now with me, and listen to my sighs,
   Ye piteous hearts, as pity bids ye do.
   Mark how they force their way out and press
      through ;
If they be once pent up, the whole life dies.
Seeing that now indeed my weary eyes
   Oftener refuse than I can tell to you
   (Even though my endless grief is ever new),

To weep and let the smothered anguish rise.
Also in sighing ye shall hear me call
  On her whose blessèd presence doth enrich
  The only home that well befitteth her :
And ye shall hear a bitter scorn of all
  Sent from the inmost of my spirit in speech
  That mourns its joy and its joy's minister.

But when I had written this sonnet, bethinking me who he was to whom I was to give it, that it might appear to be his speech, it seemed to me that this was but a poor and barren gift for one of her so near kindred. Wherefore, before giving him this sonnet, I wrote two stanzas of a poem : the first being written in very sooth as though it were spoken by him, but the other being mine own speech, albeit, unto one who should not look closely, they would both seem to be said by the same person. Nevertheless,

looking closely, one must perceive that it is not
so, inasmuch as one does not call this most gracious
creature *his lady*, and the other does, as is mani-
festly apparent. And I gave the poem and the
sonnet unto my friend, saying that I had made
them only for him.

*The poem begins, "Whatever while," and has two
parts. In the first, that is, in the first stanza, this
my dear friend, her kinsman, laments. In the second,
I lament; that is, in the other stanza, which begins,
"For ever." And thus it appears that in this poem
two persons lament, of whom one laments as a
brother, the other as a servant.*

WHATEVER while the thought comes over me
    That I may not again
      Behold that lady whom I mourn for now,
  About my heart my mind brings constantly
    So much of extreme pain

That I say, Soul of mine, why stayest thou?
Truly the anguish, Soul, that we must bow
Beneath, until we win out of this life,
  Gives me full oft a fear that trembleth :
  So that I call on Death
Even as on Sleep one calleth after strife,
  Saying, Come unto me. Life showeth grim
  And bare ; and if one dies, I envy him.

For ever, among all my sighs which burn,
  There is a piteous speech
    That clamours upon death continually :
Yea, unto him doth my whole spirit turn
  Since first his hand did reach
    My lady's life with most foul cruelty.
    But from the height of woman's fairness,
    she,
Going up from us with the joy we had,
  Grew perfectly and spiritually fair ;

That so she spreads even there
A light of Love which makes the Angels glad,
  And even unto their subtle minds can bring
  A certain awe of profound marvelling.

On that day which fulfilled the year since my lady had been made of the citizens of eternal life, remembering me of her as I sat alone, I betook myself to draw the resemblance of an angel upon certain tablets. And while I did thus, chancing to turn my head, I perceived that some were standing beside me to whom I should have given courteous welcome, and that they were observing what I did : also I learned afterwards that they had been there a while before I perceived them. Perceiving whom, I arose for salutation, and said : "Another was with me."*

* Thus according to some texts. The majority, however, add the words, "And therefore was I in thought :" but the shorter speech is perhaps the more forcible and pathetic.

Afterwards, when they had left me, I set myself again to mine occupation, to wit, to the drawing figures of angels : in doing which, I conceived to write of this matter in rhyme, as for her anniversary, and to address my rhymes unto those who had just left me. It was then that I wrote the sonnet which saith, "That lady" and as this sonnet hath two commencements, it behoveth me to divide it with both of them here.

I say that, according to the first, this sonnet has three parts. In the first, I say that this lady was then in my memory. In the second, I tell what Love therefore did with me. In the third, I speak of the effects of Love. The second begins here, "Love knowing ;" the third here, "Forth went they." This part divides into two. In the one, I say that all my sighs issued speaking. In the other, I say how some spoke certain words different from the others. The second begins here, "And still." In this same

manner is it divided with the other beginning, save
that, in the first part, I tell when this lady had thus
come into my mind, and this I say not in the other.

THAT lady of all gentle memories
    Had lighted on my soul;—whose new abode
    Lies now, as it was well ordained of God,
Among the poor in heart, where Mary is.
Love, knowing that dear image to be his,
    Woke up within the sick heart sorrow-bow'd,
    Unto the sighs which are its weary load
Saying, "Go forth." And they went forth, I wis;
Forth went they from my breast that throbbed and
      ached;
    With such a pang as oftentimes will bathe
      Mine eyes with tears when I am left alone.
And still those sighs which drew the heaviest breath
Came whispering thus : "O noble intellect!
    It is a year to-day that thou art gone."

Second Commencement.

THAT lady of all gentle memories
 Had lighted on my soul;—for whose sake flow'd
 The tears of Love; in whom the power abode
Which led you to observe while I did this.
Love, knowing that dear image to be his, etc.

Then, having sat for some space sorely in thought
because of the time that was now past, I was so
filled with dolorous imaginings that it became
outwardly manifest in mine altered countenance.
Whereupon, feeling this and being in dread lest
any should have seen me, I lifted mine eyes to
look; and then perceived a young and very beautiful
lady, who was gazing upon me from a window with
a gaze full of pity, so that the very sum of pity
appeared gathered together in her. And seeing that
unhappy persons, when they beget compassion in
others, are then most moved unto weeping, as

though they also felt pity for themselves, it came to
pass that mine eyes began to be inclined unto tears.
Wherefore, becoming fearful lest I should make
manifest mine abject condition, I rose up, and went
where I could not be seen of that lady; saying after-
wards within myself: " Certainly with her also must
abide most noble Love." And with that, I resolved
upon writing a sonnet, wherein, speaking unto her, I
should say all that I have just said. And as this
sonnet is very evident, I will not divide it :—

MINE eyes beheld the blessed pity spring
   Into thy countenance immediately
   A while agone, when thou beheldst in me
The sickness only hidden grief can bring;
And then I knew thou wast considering
   How abject and forlorn my life must be;
   And I became afraid that thou shouldst see
My weeping, and account it a base thing.

Therefore I went out from thee ; feeling how
  The tears were straightway loosened at my
    heart
  Beneath thine eyes' compassionate control.
  And afterwards I said within my soul :
"Lo ! with this lady dwells the counterpart
Of the same Love who holds me weeping now."

It happened after this, that whensoever I was
seen of this lady, she became pale and of a piteous
countenance, as though it had been with love ;
whereby she remembered me many times of my
own most noble lady, who was wont to be of a like
paleness. And I know that often, when I could
not weep nor in any way give ease unto mine anguish,
I went to look upon this lady, who seemed to bring
the tears into my eyes by the mere sight of her.
Of the which thing I bethought me to speak unto
her in rhyme, and then made this sonnet : which

begins, "Love's pallor," and which is plain without
being divided, by its exposition aforesaid :—

LOVE'S pallor and the semblance of deep ruth
   Were never yet shown forth so perfectly
   In any lady's face, chancing to see
Grief's miserable countenance uncouth,
As in thine, lady, they have sprung to soothe,
   When in mine anguish thou hast looked on me ;
   Until sometimes it seems as if, through thee,
My heart might almost wander from its truth.
Yet so it is, I cannot hold mine eyes
   From gazing very often upon thine
     In the sore hope to shed those tears they
      keep ;
And at such time, thou mak'st the pent tears rise
   Even to the brim, till the eyes waste and pine ;
   Yet cannot they, while thou art present, weep.

At length, by the constant sight of this lady, mine

eyes began to be gladdened overmuch with her
company; through which thing many times I had
much unrest, and rebuked myself as a base person :
also, many times I cursed the unsteadfastness of mine
eyes, and said to them inwardly : "Was not your
grievous condition of weeping wont one while to
make others weep? And will ye now forget this
thing because a lady looketh upon you? who so
looketh merely in compassion of the grief ye then
showed for your own blessed lady. But whatso ye
can, that do ye, accursed eyes! many a time will
I make you remember it! for never, till death dry
you up, should ye make an end of your weeping."
And when I had spoken thus unto mine eyes, I
was taken again with extreme and grievous sighing.
And to the end that this inward strife which I had
undergone might not be hidden from all saving the
miserable wretch who endured it, I proposed to
write a sonnet, and to comprehend in it this horrible

condition. And I wrote this which begins, "The very bitter weeping."

The sonnet has two parts. In the first, I speak to my eyes, as my heart spoke within myself. In the second, I remove a difficulty, showing who it is that speaks thus: and this part begins here, "So far." It well might receive other divisions also; but this would be useless, since it is manifest by the preceding exposition.

"The very bitter weeping that ye made
    So long a time together, eyes of mine,
    Was wont to make the tears of pity shine
In other eyes full oft, as I have said.
But now this thing were scarce rememberèd
    If I, on my part, foully would combine
    With you, and not recall each ancient sign
Of grief, and her for whom your tears were shed
It is your fickleness that doth betray

My mind to fears, and makes me tremble thus

What while a lady greets me with her eyes.

Except by death, we must not any way

Forget our lady who is gone from us."

So far doth my heart utter, and then sighs.

The sight of this lady brought me into so unwonted a condition that I often thought of her as of one too dear unto me; and I began to consider her thus: "This lady is young, beautiful, gentle, and wise; perchance it was Love himself who set her in my path, that so my life might find peace." And there were times when I thought yet more fondly, until my heart consented unto its reasoning. But when it had so consented, my thought would often turn round upon me, as moved by reason, and cause me to say within myself: "What hope is this which would console me after so base a fashion, and which hath taken the place of all other imagining?" Also there was another voice within me, that said: "And wilt thou, having suffered so much tribulation through Love, not escape while yet thou mayst from so much bitterness? Thou must surely know that this thought carries with it the desire of Love and drew its life from the gentle eyes of that lady who vouchsafed thee so much pity." Wherefore I, having striven sorely and very often with myself, bethought me to say somewhat thereof in rhyme. And seeing that in the battle of doubts, the victory most often remained with such as inclined towards the lady of whom I speak, it seemed to me that I should address this sonnet unto her: in the first line whereof, I call that thought which spake of her a gentle thought, only because it spoke of one who was gentle; being of itself most vile.*

* Boccaccio tells us that Dante was married to Gemma Donati about a year after the death of Beatrice. Can Gemma

In this sonnet I make myself into two, according as my thoughts were divided one from the other. The one part I call Heart, that is, appetite; the other, Soul, that is, reason; and I tell what one saith to the other. And that it is fitting to call the appetite Heart, and the reason Soul, is manifest enough to them to whom I wish this to be open. True it is that, in the preceding sonnet, I take the part of the Heart against the Eyes; and that appears contrary to what I say in the present; and therefore I say that, there also, by the Heart I mean appetite, because yet greater was my desire to remember my

then be "the lady of the window," his love for whom Dante so contemns? Such a passing conjecture (when considered together with the interpretation of this passage in Dante's later work, the *Convito*) would of course imply an admission of what I believe to lie at the heart of all true Dantesque commentary; that is, the existence always of the actual events even where the allegorical superstructure has been raised by Dante himself.

*most gentle lady than to see this other, although
indeed I had some appetite towards her, but it ap-
peared slight: wherefrom it appears that the one
statement is not contrary to the other. This sonnet
has three parts. In the first, I begin to say to this
lady how my desires turn all towards her. In the
second, I say how the Soul, that is, the reason, speaks
to the Heart, that is, to the appetite. In the third,
I say how the latter answers. The second begins
here, "And what is this?" the third here, "And
the heart answers."*

A GENTLE thought there is will often start,
   Within my secret self, to speech of thee:
   Also of Love it speaks so tenderly
That much in me consents and takes its part.
"And what is this," the soul saith to the heart,
   "That cometh thus to comfort thee and me,
   And thence where it would dwell, thus potently

Can drive all other thoughts by its strange art ?"
And the heart answers : "Be no more at strife
'Twixt doubt and doubt : this is Love's messenger
And speaketh but his words, from him received ;
And all the strength it owns and all the life
It draweth from the gentle eyes of her
Who, looking on our grief, hath often grieved."

But against this adversary of reason, there rose up in me on a certain day, about the ninth hour, a strong visible phantasy, wherein I seemed to behold the most gracious Beatrice, habited in that crimson raiment which she had worn when I had first beheld her; also she appeared to me of the same tender age as then. Whereupon I fell into a deep thought of her : and my memory ran back, according to the order of time, unto all those matters in the which she had borne a part; and my heart began painfully to repent of the desire by which it had so basely let itself be possessed during so many days, contrary to the constancy of reason.

And then, this evil desire being quite gone from me, all my thoughts turned again unto their excellent Beatrice. And I say most truly that from that hour I thought constantly of her with the whole humbled and ashamed heart; the which became often manifest in sighs, that had among them the name of that most gracious creature, and how she departed from us. Also it would come to pass very often, through the bitter anguish of some one thought, that I forgot both it, and myself, and where I was. By this increase of sighs, my weeping, which before had been somewhat lessened, increased in like manner; so that mine eyes seemed to long only for tears and to cherish them, and came at last to be circled about with red as though they had suffered martyrdom : neither were they able to look again upon the beauty of any face that might again bring them to shame and evil : from which things it will appear that they were fitly guerdoned for their unsteadfastness. Wherefore I, (wishing that mine abandonment of all such evil desires and vain temptations should be certified and made manifest, beyond all doubts which might have been suggested by the rhymes aforewritten) proposed to write a sonnet wherein I should express this purport. And I then wrote, "Woe's me !"

I said, " Woe's me !" because I was ashamed of the trifling of mine eyes. This sonnet I do not divide, since its purport is manifest enough.

WOE'S me ! by dint of all these sighs that come
    Forth of my heart, its endless grief to prove,
    Mine eyes are conquered, so that even to move
Their lids for greeting is grown troublesome.
They wept so long that now they are grief's home,
    And count their tears all laughter far above :

They wept till they are circled now by Love
With a red circle in sign of martyrdom.
These musings, and the sighs they bring from me,
  Are grown at last so constant and so sore
    That love swoons in my spirit with faint breath
Hearing in those sad sounds continually
  The most sweet name that my dead lady bore,
    With many grievous words touching her death.

About this time, it happened that a great number
of persons undertook a pilgrimage, to the end that
they might behold that blessed portraiture bequeathed
unto us by our Lord Jesus Christ as the image of
His beautiful countenance,* (upon which countenance
my dear lady now looketh continually). And certain
among these pilgrims, who seemed very thoughtful,

---

* The Veronica (*Vera icon*, or true image) ; that is, the
napkin with which a woman was said to have wiped our
Saviour's face on His way to the cross, and which miraculously

passed by a path which is well-nigh in the midst of the city where my most gracious lady was born, and abode, and at last died.

Then I, beholding them, said within myself: "These pilgrims seem to be come from very far; and I think they cannot have heard speak of this lady, or know anything concerning her. Their thoughts are not of her, but of other things; it may be, of their friends who are far distant, and whom we, in our turn, know not." And I went on to say: "I know that if they were of a country near unto

retained its likeness. Dante makes mention of it also in the *Commedia* (Parad. xxi. 103), where he says:—

> "Qual è colui che forse di Croazia
>   Viene a veder la Veronica nostra,
>   Che per l'antica fama non si sazia
>   Ma dice nel pensier fin che si mostra:
>   Signor mio Gesù Cristo, Iddio verace,
>   Or fu sì fatta la sembianza vostra?" etc.

us, they would in some wise seem disturbed, passing
through this city which is so full of grief." And I
said also: "If I could speak with them a space,
I am certain that I should make them weep before
they went forth of this city; for those things that
they would hear from me must needs beget weeping
in any."

And when the last of them had gone by me, I
bethought me to write a sonnet, showing forth
mine inward speech; and that it might seem the
more pitiful, I made as though I had spoken it indeed
unto them. And I wrote this sonnet, which
beginneth: "Ye pilgrim-folk." I made use of the
word *pilgrim* for its general signification; for
"pilgrim" may be understood in two senses, one
general, and one special. General, so far as any
man may be called a pilgrim who leaveth the
place of his birth; whereas, more narrowly speaking,
he only is a pilgrim who goeth towards or frowards

the House of St. James. For there are three
separate denominations proper unto those who
undertake journeys to the glory of God. They
are called Palmers who go beyond the seas eastward,
whence often they bring palm-branches. And
Pilgrims, as I have said, are they who journey
unto the holy House of Gallicia; seeing that no
other apostle was buried so far from his birthplace
as was the blessed Saint James. And there is a
third sort who are called Romers; in that they go
whither these whom I have called pilgrims went:
which is to say, unto Rome.

*This sonnet is not divided, because its own words
sufficiently declare it.*

　　YE pilgrim-folk, advancing pensively
　　　　As if in thought of distant things, I pray,
　　　　Is your own land indeed so far away—
　　　　As by your aspect it would seem to be—

That this our heavy sorrow leaves you free
 Though passing through the mournful town mid-
  way ;
Like unto men that understand to-day
Nothing at all of her great misery ?
Yet if ye will but stay, whom I accost,
 And listen to my words a little space,
  At going ye shall mourn with a loud voice.
It is her Beatrice that she hath lost ;
 Of whom the least word spoken holds such grace
  That men weep hearing it, and have no choice.

A while after these things, two gentle ladies sent
unto me, praying that I would bestow upon them
certain of these my rhymes. And I (taking into
account their worthiness and consideration) resolved
that I would write also a new thing, and send it
them together with those others, to the end that
their wishes might be more honourably fulfilled.

Therefore I made a sonnet, which narrates my condition, and which I caused to be conveyed to them, accompanied by the one preceding, and with that other which begins, " Stay now with me and listen to my sighs." And the new sonnet is, " Beyond the sphere."

This sonnet comprises five parts. In the first, I tell whither my thought goeth, naming the place by the name of one of its effects. In the second, I say wherefore it goeth up, and who makes it go thus. In the third, I tell what it saw, namely, a lady honoured. And I then call it a " Pilgrim Spirit," because it goes up spiritually, and like a pilgrim who is out of his known country. In the fourth, I say how the spirit sees her such (that is, in such quality) that I cannot understand her; that is to say, my thought rises into the quality of her in a degree that my intellect cannot comprehend, seeing that our intellect is, towards those blessed souls, like our eye

*weak against the sun; and this the Philosopher says
in the Second of the Metaphysics. In the fifth, I say
that, although I cannot see there whither my thought
carries me—that is, to her admirable essence—I at
least understand this, namely, that it is a thought
of my lady, because I often hear her name therein.
And, at the end of this fifth part, I say, " Ladies
mine," to show that they are ladies to whom I speak.
The second part begins, " A new perception;" the
third, " When it hath reached;" the fourth, " It sees
her such;" the fifth, " And yet I know." It might
be divided yet more nicely, and made yet clearer;
but this division may pass, and therefore I stay not
to divide it further.*

BEYOND the sphere which spreads to widest space
   Now soars the sigh that my heart sends above:
   A new perception born of grieving Love
Guideth it upward the untrodden ways.

When it hath reached unto the end, and stays,
  It sees a lady round whom splendours move
  In homage ; till, by the great light thereof
Abashed, the pilgrim spirit stands at gaze.
It sees her such, that when it tells me this
  Which it hath seen, I understand it not,
  It hath a speech so subtile and so fine.
And yet I know its voice within my thought
  Often remembereth me of Beatrice :
  So that I understand it, ladies mine.

After writing this sonnet, it was given unto me
to behold a very wonderful vision : * wherein I saw

* This we may believe to have been the Vision of Hell,
Purgatory, and Paradise, which furnished the triple argument
of the *Divina Commedia*. The Latin words ending the
Vita Nuova are almost identical with those at the close of
the letter in which Dante, on concluding the *Paradise*, and
accomplishing the hope here expressed, dedicates his great
work to Can Grande della Scala.

things which determined me that I would say nothing further of this most blessed one, until such time as I could discourse more worthily concerning her. And to this end I labour all I can; as she well knoweth. Wherefore if it be His pleasure through whom is the life of all things, that my life continue with me a few years, it is my hope that I shall yet write concerning her what hath not before been written of any woman. After the which, may it seem good unto Him who is the Master of Grace, that my spirit should go hence to behold the glory of its lady: to wit, of that blessed Beatrice who now gazeth continually on His countenance *qui est per omnia sæcula benedictus.* * *Laus Deo.*

* " Who is blessed throughout all ages."

THE END.

CPSIA information can be obtained at www.ICGtesting.com
Printed in the USA
LVOW012000131212

311556LV00028B/1242/P